THE
SECRET
PLACE OF
THUNDER

THE
SECRET
PLACE OF
THUNDER

Trading Our Need to Be
Noticed for a
Hidden Life with Christ

JOHN STARKE

ZONDERVAN
REFLECTIVE

ZONDERVAN REFLECTIVE

The Secret Place of Thunder
Copyright © 2023 by John Starke

Requests for information should be addressed to:
Zondervan, *3900 Sparks Dr. SE, Grand Rapids, Michigan 49546*

Zondervan titles may be purchased in bulk for educational, business, fundraising, or sales promotional use. For information, please email SpecialMarkets@Zondervan.com.

ISBN 978-0-310-13984-3 (softcover)
ISBN 978-0-310-13986-7 (audio)
ISBN 978-0-310-13985-0 (ebook)

Published in association with the literary agent Don Gates @ THEGATESGROUP.

Cover design: Emily Weigel Design
Cover art: © Pawel Czerwinski / Unsplash
Interior design: Sara Colley

Printed in the United States of America

HB 04.19.2024

To
Corinne, Owen,
Noelle, and Ryland

CONTENTS

INTRODUCTION

Several weeks into the COVID-19 pandemic, I received a call from a troubled member of our church community. She explained that she had a project due at work in two weeks, yet because her directors weren't going to see her work until then, she found herself anxiously doing loads of smaller projects in the meantime and turning them in. She admitted that her bosses were not expecting these smaller projects. She didn't know whether they were using these projects, but she needed the assurance that they saw her being productive. But it was exhausting, since she still needed to give a significant amount of time to the project that *was* assigned to her. "I guess I didn't realize how much I depended on being noticed," she said.

As I got off the phone, I thought, *This is a pattern.* My pastoral counseling calls were beginning to take a common shape. I was a bit surprised at people's deep anxiety, not about health or safety (though that was present), but about being invisible to their bosses and supervisors at work. Suddenly, due to a life-altering virus, we were all thrown into isolated lives we didn't know how to live. Everyone was now working from home. Midtown Manhattan office buildings were emptied out and the streets became quiet. Our lives were suddenly hidden. And many began to fear the consequences of not being seen.

I wasn't sure how to approach these moments of pastoral care. I sensed a dynamic at work that I didn't know how to put into words. Something was humming under the hood of our hearts that COVID-19 didn't create but had simply exposed. Whatever it was, I could tell it was deeply entrenched in our broader culture and had insidiously wormed its way into the church.

Performative Individualism

After taking part in many conversations, listening, reading, reflecting, and researching, I began to see the shape of this alarming dynamic a little more clearly. I realized that our culture had taken a step beyond what sociologist Robert Bellah calls *expressive individualism*, a belief that our identity is formed by self-expression as we discover our deepest desires and carry them out as an expression of our authentic selves.[1] Bellah, in the 1980s, argued that this form of individualism defined our modern Western culture. This, of course, conflicted with how Christianity understands our identity—namely, that we do not create an identity out of our self-expression but receive one in Christ.

Yet I think our culture has evolved beyond mere expressive individualism into something a bit more sinister—into *performative individualism*. Inward-focused self-expression has subtly turned into a demanding cultural expectation. The shift is likely more easily felt than articulated, but consider how we experience relationships. As Bellah describes it, relationships in the latter half of the twentieth century began to center around self-expression more than personal commitments. This, of course, caused relationships to become somewhat superficial. We might treat relationships (or church commitments) the same way we would treat a gym membership. We commit to the gym as long as it serves what we want to see in ourselves. But if it no longer serves that end, we cancel our membership. If our relationships are enhancing our sense of self, we happily stick around. But when relationships begin to demand that we change or sacrifice, our commitment to those relationships will diminish or we will even leave.

But in recent years, relationships have become more performative. Instead of seeing relationships merely as part of our self-expression, we now feel the pressure and necessity not only to affirm the self-expression of others (especially as it relates to sexuality), but also to live and speak in ways that affirm and are consistent with the self-expression of others. If not, the consequences involve not only losing the relationship but also being seen as ignorant or even evil.

I wasn't the first to notice these developments. Researchers are finding that young adults today "are perceiving that their social context is increasingly demanding, that others judge them more harshly, and that they are increasingly inclined to *display perfection* as a means of securing approval."[2] In other words, our culture supports individual expressions of a self-curated identity. However, if our self-expression doesn't meet certain socially constructed expectations, we will be ignored, isolated, dismissed, or canceled. We want to be ourselves, but we also want to be loved. Our culture rarely allows us both.

The anxiety I witnessed in my church members of "not being seen" was a new expression of something deeper that already existed in our culture. Many of us have internalized the idea that the markers of "being okay," of having an admirable life and enviable success, are primarily visible. Performance has become more important than reality.[3]

Sophie Gilbert, TV critic for *The Atlantic*, explains why

shows like the Netflix series *Tidying Up with Marie Kondo* and others are so popular. It's not simply that young adults now prefer minimalism over the consumeristic collection of "stuff" of their parents; it's that we need the *right* stuff that shows we have the *right* taste in order to achieve an enviable life.[4] The promise, writes Gilbert, "is that if people work to organize their lives to look just right, the rest will follow." We live as if the most important things about us should be performed before others, as if our deepest happiness will come from being who others think we ought to be.

This contemporary dynamic has ancient roots. The Old and New Testaments warn against fearing man more than God. We have known about this impulse since Adam, but like all ancient problems, this one has taken a modern shape. For example, 81 percent of those born in the 1980s report that getting materially rich is one of their top goals in life. This figure is 20 percent higher than for those born in the 1960s and '70s. But more recent generations over the same life period borrow more heavily and "spend, on average, a far greater proportion of income on status possessions and image goods than did their parents."[5] In other words, there is a preoccupation with the perception of things. We "overvalue performance and undervalue the self."[6]

Our Instagram posts display balanced and successful lives, but under the surface is a deep frailty. Research shows associations between performance-driven individualism and clinical depression, eating disorders, early death, and suicidal ideation, especially among college students and younger adults.[7]

And this cultural phenomenon isn't limited to secular spaces. It has also shaped how many of us within the church practice our faith. I wonder if you sense this. The most obvious place this is played out is online—on social media—where we can display when and where we practice our morning devotions or give some public assurance that our beliefs and actions are on the right side of history. These posts can be innocent, of course. But they can also be driven by a fear of being forgotten or ignored, of being aligned with the canceled, or by a desire to impress others. This is how many of us are shaping our identity and forming our sense of self. Much of the time, we aren't even aware we're doing it.

Social media tends to be the most conspicuous arena where this plays out, but it's not the most significant. The reason researchers call this a "cultural phenomenon" is that, in many ways, it defines how we live our lives. This is how we do relationships, how we pursue our vocations, how we think about money, how we consume media, and, of course, how we practice spirituality. It runs more deeply than we think. If you are a spiritual leader, maybe you are connecting the dots of how this is working out in the lives of those in your spiritual community. It may also be shaping the way you lead.

Practicing Righteousness

As we've seen, our culture teaches us that the most important things about us are what can be performed before others. Jesus, on the other hand, teaches us that the most important things about us are practiced in secret. "Beware of practicing your righteousness before other people in order to be seen by them," Jesus says in Matthew 6:1. This comes in the middle of his Sermon on the Mount, where he is working out a principle that doesn't just guard against self-righteousness but provides a strategy for spiritual renewal. If our performative culture has led to disintegrated inner lives, then Jesus provides a path toward wholeness.

In the previous passage (Matthew 5:17–48), Jesus worked through a number of sins (murder, adultery, divorce) to show that there's a sin behind each sin—anger behind murder, lust behind adultery. In chapter 6, Jesus begins to look at a number of virtues (almsgiving, fasting, and prayer), and now he is concerned about the sin behind each virtue: Don't practice your righteousness before others.

Jesus says, "Beware." He is explaining that this can trip you up; it can surprise you. It is an ordinary temptation, not an extraordinary one. Beware of practicing your righteousness, showcasing your wisdom, performing your faith before others where you can be seen. Because the longer you are in faith communities, the more you learn what it *looks like* to be humble—what facial expression to make, how to carry yourself, what words to say, how to be seen without looking like you want to be seen. The longer you are a Christian, the more believable you can be. You get good at it.

There's sobriety to Jesus' words. He warns us that for those who live out this performative life, trying to display their good lives for others to see, "Truly . . . they have received their reward" (Matthew 6:2). He wants us to grasp the flimsiness of the reward. You get what you want, but it is not satisfying. Human recognition and praise come with a jolt of attention that makes you feel good, but it is fleeting and fickle. So often our aspirations don't go beyond the applause or attention of others. There is a frailty to human approval, and those who seek it become frail themselves.

We have likely been catechized and shaped by a performative society more than we know. Our social systems and institutions—including our workplaces and even the church—reward performance. As Yuval Levin puts it, "We have moved, roughly speaking, from thinking of institutions as molds that shape people's character and habits toward seeing them as platforms that allow people to be themselves and to display themselves before a wider world."[8] Instead of places to be formed, institutions have become places to perform.

But Jesus comes from outside the systems and institutions of this world. In Matthew 6 and other portions of the Gospels, he works out a way to grow out of frailty into spiritual vibrancy. Jesus teaches us to aim our lives toward the "Father who sees in secret" (Matthew 6:4).

This ancient spiritual principle of hiddenness feels foreign to us. We instinctively work to live publicly and performatively. The way of Christ seems fruitless to modern people. If no one sees our efforts, how are we to make a difference? How are we to be loved? But Jesus and other New Testament writers show us that there is a spiritual potency to hiddenness. We might call it a fruitful dormancy.

Fruitful Dormancy

This isn't a book on escapism or living a more secluded or private life. Actually, it's about how to live more fruitfully with others. In Edwin Friedman's book *A Failure of Nerve*, he explains that what brings healing to a toxic system is not primarily someone's gifts or intelligence or leadership capacities. What truly counts, he says, is "a non-anxious presence."[9]

My father is an artist, and I grew up watching him paint in

his studio. Every day, I would find him working there from early in the morning until late in the evening. I loved watching him work. I remember one day bringing a few friends down to his studio to show them his paintings. I was a teenager and wanted my friends to be as impressed with my dad as I was.

As we entered the studio, he was just starting a new painting. They were going to see how the magic happened!

As my dad began, he sketched out the shape of the painting using neutral colors and broad strokes. It was messy and chaotic. There was no color yet, no detail. I was getting anxious. This was taking a while, and it looked like something a child could draw. I could sense that my friends were not very impressed. I wanted my dad to hurry up and make it beautiful. But my dad's face didn't reveal any of the anxiety I felt as he painted. He knew where it was going and how to make it beautiful.

Jesus, who is working in this world, is not anxious. He knows where all of this is going, and he knows how to make something beautiful. The New Testament gives us a principle of hiddenness that still encourages non-anxious participation in this world with Christ. Hiddenness is not hiding; it is living fundamentally before the Father, who "sees in secret" and gives more satisfying rewards than those offered by the world (Matthew 6:4).

When Jesus says his Father sees in secret and gives us rewards, he's not describing a transactional dynamic. Jesus is pointing out a contrast of rewards—attention from others (whatever that may grant you) versus attention from God. Jesus would stop us short of saying our glory in heaven will increase the more we do righteousness in secret. This isn't a "the more you do the more you'll get" relationship. No, the reward is being seen by God, our Father.

Jesus is decommercializing our rewards through family dynamics. He is alluding to our deep longings for a father. We all want to be seen. We all want to be noticed.

From our childhood, we've all been crying out, "Look at me!" When a baby is born, nurses expect to hear the baby cry; otherwise, something might be physically wrong. A baby's need to be noticed is a matter of survival. Jesus is not saying, "You need to get rid of that desire." It's just that our healthy desire to be seen has become disordered.

Jesus teaches us a better way. In Luke 3, Jesus is baptized, inaugurating his public life and ministry. This starts with a word from the Father, not the affirmation of others. As Jesus is lowered into the water and brought back up, the heavens open and God the Father says over Jesus, "You are my beloved Son; with you I am well pleased" (v. 22).

Jesus knew that the affirmation and attention of other people would be fickle and would never sustain him. No lasting reward was to be found there. The people who would praise him one minute would shout, "Crucify him!" the next. He needed to hear the voice of the Father speaking affirmation that was infinite, unwavering, and pure. No mixed motives. Absolute steadfast and sustaining love.

In this life, you will hear voices you will not want to disappoint—some from your own heart, others from past or current relationships, and some from your culture. You will want to impress them and receive affirmation from them. Our world teaches us to form our identity based on what these voices say. But they are all fickle, easily disappointed and easily distracted by other things.

In Matthew 6, Jesus pushes us to seek the voice of the Father.

If you are a Christian, you are in God's family. What belongs to Christ belongs to you. Therefore, you have a better reward than empty and short-term validation. You have a Father who says, "You are my beloved daughter, you are my beloved son, and in you I am well pleased." Nothing is better than that.

But as we'll see in the next chapter, there may be some things we need to outgrow in order to have a more experiential grasp of the Father's voice.

Chapter 1

PERFORMATIVE SPIRITUALITY

A merican pop culture has teased us," writes Terry Nguyễn, "with this carefree notion of youth—that you should be binge-drinking every other weekend or taking spontaneous international trips. And what's incredibly maddening for young people is that, during our most formative years, the only thing we can focus on is survival."[1] Nguyễn is a journalist for *Vox* who covers the challenges and struggles of young adulthood in a digital era. Here, she's describing a generation of young adults who had to figure out their vocational trajectories amid both the 2008 recession and the 2020 pandemic.[2] These young adults feel tremendous cultural pressure to have visual indicators of success in a time when it is exceptionally difficult to gain them.

Journalist Anne Helen Petersen, who has written quite a bit about millennials and why their experience of burnout is so widespread, writes that we post images online, attempting not only to show others that our lives are successful and balanced but to convince ourselves! "We all know," she writes, "what we see on Facebook and Instagram isn't 'real,' but that doesn't mean we don't judge ourselves against it." But we as a culture may not have the resources to do otherwise. Petersen continues:

> I find that millennials are far less jealous of objects or belongings on social media than the holistic experiences represented there, the sort of thing that prompts people to comment, *I want your life*. That enviable mix of leisure and travel, the

accumulation of pets and children, the landscapes inhabited and the food consumed seems not just desirable, but balanced, satisfied, and unafflicted by burnout.[3]

As Sophie Gilbert points out, a show like Marie Kondo's *Tidying Up* syncs "with its cultural moment, a time in which identity and achievement are visual metrics to be displayed and curated, and a happy home is a perfected, optimized one."[4] This widely shared experience is what researchers call a "cultural phenomenon." It's in the air we breathe. It's a social catechism we're all digesting, where a young adult "only learns through performance that he has a self," feeling pressured to "procure others' approval and repair feelings of unworthiness and shame through displays of high achievement."[5] In this cultural phenomenon, the performance of the self is more important than the reality of the self.

Petersen reflects on how her university and graduate students have felt the pressure of finding a good first job, saying they were convinced it "would not only determine their career trajectory, but also their intrinsic value for the rest of their lives." Our society casts a big vision of young adults finding "employment that reflects well on their parents (steady, decently paying, recognizable as a 'good job') that's also impressive to their peers (at a 'cool' company) and fulfills what they've been *told* has been the end goal of all of this childhood optimization: doing work that you're passionate about."[6]

In the last few years, journalists and researchers have shown that modern people reach for healing ("repair feelings of unworthiness and shame") and gain a sense of self-worth ("career trajectory" and "intrinsic value") through performance. And yet we see evidence of how this performative life doesn't work functionally in our modern world.

Jesus shows that a performative life has always been destructive spiritually. This impulse toward performative living isn't new, or else Jesus wouldn't have warned against it in the Sermon on the Mount. But it has taken on a modern shape. Therefore, some ancient pathways are needed to help us toward wholeness.

The Safety of Performance

As I sit with people in our church community, time and time again I hear about an unspoken pressure to live up to certain visions of a "balanced" life—with the kinds of vacations, leisure activities, and social life they believe measure up to an "admirable life." One friend of mine had to confess anger with her husband because he wanted to post a picture of her in their kitchen that, in its current state of run-down cabinetry and outdated appliances, didn't portray the kind of success they had hoped for at this point in life. She felt embarrassed admitting this out loud, but at the same time, she began to recognize how our culture had formed her toward more performative patterns.

As a pastor, I feel sad watching those around me live with the illusions of what they think people expect of them. Even more, these illusions are startling to see in myself. Now into my forties, I find there are kinds of travel and experiences, competencies in parenting, and vocational accomplishments as a pastor I haven't reached, and I see at times my impulse to compensate for these weaknesses or limitations. David Benner says we have internalized the belief that our deepest happiness will come from being who others think we ought to be rather than from living the way God views us.[7]

One reason this calls for some pastoral sensitivity is that sometimes our performance comes from wounds we've received. We often become the objects of other people's hatred and insecurities. So we learn how to stay safe in an environment that doesn't allow or incentivize us to be ourselves. You might call these defense mechanisms our "safety schemes."

In times of stress, maybe we've learned how to *be in control*, like the parent who imposes layer upon layer of defenses and order to keep the unpredictable or unexpected from intruding into their life. Or in relational chaos, we *escape*, like the person who resists having difficult conversations or confronting bad behavior in others. Some try to *keep it light*, lest we feel the emotional pain we've been resisting for years.

These safety schemes buffer us from the ditches and dangers of other people's sins, but they also come impulsively from wounds and fears that need healing. These safety schemes can desensitize us to the love of Christ. They may shield us from the pain, but they also keep us from wholeness. They are evidences of the internalized message that I cannot simultaneously be myself and be loved.

Unfortunately, these are safety schemes *apart* from the love of Christ. A life that resists these schemes aims, as Paul tells us in Ephesians, to be "rooted and grounded" in the love of Christ and to "know the love of Christ" in a way that "surpasses knowledge, that you may be filled with all the fullness of God" (Ephesians 3:17, 19). For some of us, those verses come with such familiarity that our eyes glide over the words. Instead, pause and linger slowly over what Paul is trying to get us to grasp.

Paul wants us to move past merely explaining the love of Christ in an intelligent way or even pointing to examples of Christ's love in the gospel. Instead, Paul is concerned with knowing the love of Christ in a transformational way. In order to know the love of Christ and be healed by it, we must receive it in "an *undefended state*."[8] But our performative lives actively resist being undefended. In our past, a lack of defense brought so many wounds, so much pain, so much embarrassment and humiliation. Yet it is the only way to truly experience love, especially divine love. We have been shaped to perform for likes, but we do not know how to be loved.

The New Testament Gospels, however, are hopeful narratives that calmly invite us to both understand God's love and learn how to receive it. The longer I am a Christian, the more I see that we are not as vulnerable to his love as we think (more on that later), and confronting this particular shadow is more transformative than we often realize. I'm grateful Jesus has compassion on those of us who have internalized the belief that our deepest happiness comes from being who others think we ought to be. It's an exhausting life, but it's often the only one we know how to live in order to feel safe in this world.

Trumpeting Our Virtues

As an alternative, Jesus comes with words of wisdom and guidance: "Beware of practicing your righteousness before other people in order to be seen by them" (Matthew 6:1). He is warning us that the human heart has an impulse to trumpet itself. We want to be seen and admired. It's how we have learned to seek love.

Cleverly, Jesus doesn't just warn us against showing off our riches, our skill sets, or our balanced lives. Instead, he warns against the more spiritual danger of trumpeting our *virtues*. He gives three examples: giving to the poor, praying, and fasting. He says that when you give to the poor, "sound no trumpet before you" (Matthew 6:2). Don't draw attention to yourself. Instead, give in secret so that the only one who knows is the Father (v. 4).

Or when you pray (Matthew 6:5–8), don't give wordy, loud prayers. Jesus warns against the example of those who loved to be seen praying in public (v. 5) and who "heap up empty phrases" (v. 7), as if God is just waiting for the right combination of words. Jesus leads us away from using words that have no connection between our mouth and our heart. You are not heard by God for your "many words"; you're heard because he loves you. You are not heard because your prayers are compelling; your Father already knows what you need. Instead, when you pray, go to your inner room, close the door, and pray to the Father "in secret" (v. 6).

The last virtue Jesus mentions here is fasting. It's the most dramatic example. He warns against fasting so others might notice (Matthew 6:16–18). When you fast, don't disfigure your face, Jesus says. It's that subtle ability we have to posture ourselves ever so slightly in a way that makes others come to us and ask, "Are you okay?" so we can respond, "Oh yeah. I'm fine. *I'm just fasting.*" Don't do this. Instead, Jesus says, when you fast, "anoint your head and wash your face" (v. 17). Jesus commands us to do the things we would normally do after we've eaten—wash our faces and anoint our heads. When you fast, he says, fool others into thinking you're eating.

Do you see what Jesus is pointing out? When you are fasting, be careful what your disposition is telling others. Don't disfigure your face; wash it. Don't look miserable; look like you just ate. Is Jesus teaching us to be a bit misleading, even hypocritical in some way—*I know the inside of your body is miserable, but I want your face to give the impression that you're doing great?*

Jesus here is providing a principle that covers not just fasting, but all virtues. Who are these virtues for? Fasting is not for those who can see our face, but for the one who can see our heart. Don't miss this principle. Jesus is a teacher of the heart, and he's always getting us to think more deeply about the posture of our hearts rather than just the moral precision of our actions. Jesus is pointing to a deeper work that teaches us to resist a performative life altogether.

Do you know how to live, not for those who can see your face, but for the one who can see your heart? Matthew 6 teaches us about a *fast within a fast*. On the one hand, you're fasting from food, trying to stir and sustain your appetite for God. But on the other hand, you're fasting from the glory and praise of others. Don't underestimate the small crucifying power of doing things for and with God in secret, intentionally resisting praise that expands and puffs up your ego.

Repeated in Matthew 6 in verses 4, 6, and 18 is the phrase "and your Father who *sees in secret* will reward you" (emphasis mine). Twice the Father is described as the one "who is in secret" (vv. 6, 18). There's a mystery here worth meditating on. The Father sees and knows all things. But he seems to be indifferent to what we do to dazzle others. And even more deeply, he seems concerned with how we behave in order to find an identity and a sense of self-worth in this world. He wants us to see our public displays of virtue as toils that bring no lasting reward. It's laboring for bread that doesn't keep.

Life with the Father happens in a secret place, and our performative lives have no place there. Practice your virtues, Jesus urges us, and live your life primarily for the one who sees not the face but the heart. And when he sees the heart, he, of course, sees everything we'd like to hide behind our performances.

We have been taught to acknowledge and display only the most acceptable parts of ourselves. It's the way we feel safe and successful in this world. But the Father, who sees in secret, sees us all the way to the bottom and loves us to the skies. And because Jesus loves us and truly wants us to be happy, he is trying to get us to live in that secret place. Set your heart there.

The Beatitude Life

We have been living as if the most important things about us are what we perform before others, and it's making us miserable and anxious. Jesus tells us that the most important things in life are done in secret, before the Father, who loves us simply because he loves us.

One counterargument to this might go like this: "Yes, but doesn't Jesus also say, 'Let your light shine before others, so that they may see your good works and give glory to your Father who is in heaven'" (Matthew 5:16)? Yes, he does. Why, then, would he say just a few passages later (in the same sermon!) that we ought to practice our good works in secret? Which is it—practice your life in public to be seen by others, or resist that line of thinking and keep your life secret before God?

On the surface, these two verses seem to contradict each other. Either Jesus forgot what he just said and is confused, or he is misleading us and shouldn't be trusted. Well, don't worry—there's a third option.

When Jesus tells us to practice our lives in secret, he is talking about our virtues—giving to the poor, praying, and fasting; things we might be tempted to perform before others to look impressive. But in Matthew 5:16, when he calls us to shine our works before others in such a way that they'll see and glorify God, he has just finished unveiling the Beatitudes (vv. 3–12): Blessed are the poor in spirit, those who are meek, those who mourn, those who are persecuted, those who hunger and thirst for righteousness, and those who are slandered for Christ's sake.

You can give to the poor, pray, and fast outwardly, but inwardly the substance of your life can still be based on pretense. You can do all these wonderful acts of virtue and still be a hypocrite. But poverty of spirit, mourning, meekness, joy in suffering, and endurance of slander form substance that is deeper than outward impressiveness. Living this beatitude life will produce a kind of attraction that glorifies God rather than you. In other words, it's hard to *perform* the Beatitudes. Jesus isn't concerned about performative meekness; he's concerned about performative prayer and performative justice.

But the Beatitudes Jesus describes in Matthew 5:3–12 do not just grow from nowhere. A heart that can rejoice in slander must first learn to resist the praise of others and live in secret with the Father. Jesus lived out this pattern in his own life. In John 2:1–11, after he turned water into wine at the wedding at Cana and performed many great signs, a large crowd began to believe in and follow him (v. 23). But John's gospel shows us how Jesus responded: "But Jesus on his part did not entrust himself to them, because he knew all people" (v. 24).

We tend to think this verse is primarily about what's inside a person. And it certainly is about that! The rest of John's gospel shows the frailty of our beliefs. But it also reveals what's inside Jesus: He "did not entrust himself to them." Jesus knew how to practice the principle of Matthew 6, resisting the world's praise. He entrusted himself to something deeper than man's approval—a deeper reward, so to speak. It's almost as if Jesus is singing Psalm 102 to himself: "They will perish, but you will remain; they will all wear out like a garment . . . You are the same, and your years have no end" (vv. 26–27).

If you consider the end of John's gospel when the praises of man were no more and the people cried, "Crucify him!" and wanted to exchange his life for that of Barabbas, Jesus could quietly embrace the cross because his life never depended on the praise of others. And so when Jesus calls us to deny ourselves, take up our cross, and follow him (Matthew 16:24), this pattern of *not entrusting ourselves to others* must be deep within us.

Do you see? Jesus had a heart that could endure the cross and be slandered for righteousness' sake because his heart was hidden in secret with the Father who loved him. The heart that takes these small crucifying steps of learning how to resist praise from others can be formed into a heart that follows Christ—even (or especially) when it costs us deeply.

I want to emphasize that these are *small* crucifying steps. The work of unwinding our hearts is difficult and slow. It's remarkable that in the Sermon on the Mount, Jesus doesn't instruct us toward grand or famous acts of faith and courage, just ordinary spiritual obedience done in a hidden way. But even so, practicing these ordinary things—these small crucifying steps—in a hidden, intentional way has a transformative effect.

Self-Righteousness

Jesus goes one step further: "But when you give to the needy, do not let your left hand know what your right hand is doing" (Matthew 6:3). That's a strange phrase. In college, I washed windows part-time. I mostly washed the storefronts of strip malls, but every once in a while, a family friend would ask if I would wash the windows of their home. One family asked me to wash the huge windows in back of their home that faced the Catalina Mountains in Tucson, Arizona. As I was finishing, the husband came over and handed me some cash—a good bit less than what I normally charged. Sensing this slight, the wife came over quietly and discreetly handed me another twenty dollars, saying, "Don't let the left hand know what the right hand is doing." While her interpretation of Matthew 6:3 was shaky, I appreciated the extra bump.

But Jesus is encouraging us to do something deeper here. He calls us to resist practicing our righteousness not only before others but also before our own selves! There should be no external trumpets, but there should be no internal trumpets either. Bible commentator Frederick Bruner says that Jesus is trying to teach us to be "unself-conscious and unself-impressed."[9] Why? Because we often try to justify ourselves even to our own hearts. Jesus is instructing us to give to the poor without others seeing it and to do our best to keep it from inflating our own ego.

But why be so picky? Does it feel like Jesus is causing us to overanalyze every step? Why do we have to worry so much about motives? If the poor are being served, who cares about the reason behind it!

Well, if we aren't careful about motives, especially when it comes to matters concerning justice and the marginalized, the poor can become just a means to our feelings of self-justification. Justice itself becomes performative. We end up doing just enough to feel better about ourselves or to post pictures of it online rather than genuinely serving communities through sacrificial love and solidarity. This is a truth to ponder slowly in our own lives. Even as we express opinions publicly about matters concerning the poor or racial justice, are we doing so to ensure we are included on the right side and protected from being identified with the "ignorant" other side? Even as we take time out of our week to serve the poor and needy—whether working at a local shelter, doing after-school tutoring, or helping ex-inmates plot out a path to getting a job—Jesus is emphasizing the need to pay attention to our motives. This isn't a call to navel-gazing but to the spiritually important work of outgrowing any residue of safety schemes and salvation plans and developing a deeper love for the poor, which the Scriptures consistently mark as godlike (see Matthew 25:40).

Even more personally, Jesus is trying to liberate us from having to impress others and ourselves. That's a hard battle. We are constantly in this inner-outer war:

With ourselves: Am I doing okay?
With others: Do you think I'm doing okay?

We are consistently pulled either toward inner trumpets, exercising our gifts and giving our resources not primarily out of love of God and neighbor but out of a need to feel justified and impressive to ourselves, or toward outer trumpets, striving to impress others and constantly living into what we assume others think our lives ought to be like. In the next chapter, we'll see some of the destructive impact this has on the lives of teens and young adults, but also just how fragile we are becoming.

Jesus wants to free us from this pull toward inner and outer trumpets. Even more, he wants to heal us from it. He is trying to teach us to live, not for the eyes of others or even for ourselves, but in the secret place where our Father sees and rewards.

The Secret Place of Thunder

A handful of years back, my emotional life took a deep dive into a dark depression for about eighteen months. It was likely a combination of physiological things and some relational conflicts that were very painful. I had friends who were helping me stay spiritually grounded, but I remember feeling very alone and isolated. I was worried this was how I would always be—my kids always experiencing me as sad. Someone mentioned to me in passing that "it won't always be this way." But I didn't believe them. The darkness seemed definitive. There were days when I was relieved to end the day and grieved to wake up. I did not understand what was happening.

It was a long wilderness—not forty years in a literal wilderness, but I felt as if there were no tabernacle presence abiding with me. I experienced both inner darkness and outer turmoil. The relational conflict was difficult to bear and hard to make sense of. I was slandered, and my reputation was questioned by people I cherished. This, of course, led to losing some connections with friends who might have been a source of help and encouragement. Finding intimacy with others during that time was complicated.

During that season, the desire to perform was strong. As a pastor, I found it humiliating to lead with emotional weakness at that time. I wanted to give the impression of strength but had little ability to pull it off. I can count that as a grace years later. During that time, the idea that others would experience me as weak felt threatening to me. But I just didn't have much available to me to even try to create some parody of strength. It's not that I had the spiritual maturity to set aside my safety schemes; they just simply weren't available to me. Jesus was putting me (because I likely wasn't going to do it myself) in an undefended state in order for me to receive his love.

One of those days, I was sitting in my living room early in the morning and praying. Prayer wasn't easy for me in that season, but an older friend had taught me some ways to pray in the midst of pain that have helped me ever since. I was praying from Psalm 81, which is written in the voice of the Lord, reminding the Israelites that he had delivered them from slavery in Egypt:

> I relieved your shoulder of the burden;
>> your hands were freed from the basket.
> In distress you called, and I delivered you;
>> I answered you in the secret place of thunder;
>> I tested you at the waters of Meribah.
>> (Psalm 81:6–7)

"The secret place of thunder" was where he heard and answered them. The Father, who hears in secret (Matthew 6:6), listened to their cries for relief. He was their salvation. The secret place of thunder was their hope. No other place mattered.

The Lord delivered them from Egypt and brought them

through the wilderness, warning them, "There shall be no strange god among you; you shall not bow down to a foreign god" (Psalm 81:9). Resist other safety schemes. Strange gods don't take the same form nowadays as temples, icons, and sacrifices, but they stick to the same schemes of manipulating the desires and cravings of our hearts. They seem trustworthy and reasonable. The Israelites were tempted to go back to Egypt. Later they were tempted to trust in Syria to save them from Babylon. There will always be some god or goddess that offers us sensible plans to stay safe in the world but extends no true salvation or relief.

> I am the LORD your God,
>> who brought you up out of the land of Egypt.
>> Open your mouth wide, and I will fill it.
>> (Psalm 81:10)

This strange verse promises satisfaction if we will just resist the safety schemes and promises of the strange gods among us. God promises to "feed you with the finest of the wheat, and with honey from the rock I would satisfy you" (Psalm 81:16). We grasp for paths and promises that desensitize us to his love, but if we will come in an undefended state ("open your mouth wide"), he will fill us.

I don't know what my heart was feeling as I sat in my chair, drinking my coffee, trying my best to meditate on this psalm, but when I read that line—"Open your mouth wide, and I will fill it"—the words felt like a burning bush. I began to weep, and something in me wanted so badly to experience whatever this sentence was offering. My prayers sounded more like moans, but the Spirit had promised to intercede and articulate the words my moans couldn't. And somewhere in the secret place of thunder, God heard me and answered. I saw no visions and heard no voices, but I deeply sensed his presence like a warm, heavy weight. I felt like I couldn't move. I didn't want to. I desperately did not want whatever was happening to me to stop.

Pleasure. Fire. Life. Bread. Honey from the rock. I don't have clear, complete sentences to explain what the Lord offered me that day. I was a year into a dark depression, and this experience did not heal me completely. I still walked in shadows and darkness for a few more months. But that moment was a witness, and Psalm 81 has been a memorial ever since. God met me in the wilderness. He heard me in the secret place of thunder. He fed me with the finest of wheat. "Can God spread a table in the wilderness?" (Psalm 78:19). Yes, he can.

In some ways, that moment taught me again how to pray, how to set aside the things that desensitize me to God's love and distance me from his presence. My heart is creative in finding new ways to numb myself, like a think tank of safety schemes that ultimately just leave me empty rather than spurring me to open my mouth wide for him. But Jesus offers these old paths of renewal, and Psalm 81 is a personal reminder to me to resist the performative life. It won't work. Here's the truth I have learned: A performative life might lead others, at least momentarily, to think you are impressive or give you a brief sense that you are going to be okay. But these benefits are fleeting. It will not lead to a deep and abiding sense of God's presence, an experiential grasp of his love, and healing from your insecurities, anxieties, and grief. You cannot perform your way out of depression.

Maybe my experience can be a witness to you. Pray, fast, and labor for the poor in secret ways, so the Father, who sees from the secret place of thunder, can satisfy you. Let those small crucifying steps be a path toward making all of life less performative and more fundamentally hidden. And as we'll see in the next chapter, I don't think Jesus would find it an exaggeration to say it's the *only way* to truly live.

Chapter 2

A HIDDEN LIFE

When Terrence Malick's *A Hidden Life* was released, there were very few showings in New York, but my wife and I found one in a small Lower East Side theater on a Friday afternoon. The theater had maybe thirty to fifty seats, and the only other people there were an elderly couple in the very front row.

The film tells the story of an Austrian farmer, Franz Jägerstätter, who was called up to fight in World War II but refused to take a loyalty oath to Adolf Hitler. This proves to be costly not only to him but also to his family and small community. When the movie ended, we left the theater and took a long, quiet walk up 2nd Avenue. My imagination was fixed on the consistent pushback Franz received from his community, his lawyer, and even his family for resisting Hitler.

Franz was a nobody. He was a poor farmer. His life had little consequence to the world around him. Throughout the film, he was regularly asked, "Do you think your resistance will change anything?" The obvious answer was no, and the implication for his critics was that since his resistance would have no consequence, it wouldn't be worth the cost. Yet despite the cost and the loneliness of his convictions, Franz resisted.

About a year later, we wanted our kids to see the movie. Beforehand, I did a quick search to try to remember if there was any difficult or mature content. One site that gave ratings based on how much violent or sexual content was in the movie also rated the film's level of "Positive Role Models." I assumed the rating would be high for that particular category. But to my surprise, the site gave it a 2 out of 5 rating, explaining, "Franz is something of a role model, given that standing up for what he believes in takes tremendous courage, and he risks everything. But at the same time, very little change/result comes of it."[1]

The critique of Franz's character sounds ironically similar to his critics within the film itself. The quality of his virtue was measured primarily based on the results it brought.

A Mustard Seed Dynamic

Our culture is skeptical of hidden virtue. As we discussed in chapter 1, our culture incentivizes and rewards primarily performative lives. And our hearts have been formed to go along with this program. Part of growing up in Christ in today's world is to intentionally resist this way of living.

James writes about the nature of this conflict when he confronts worldliness in the fourth chapter of his letter. "Friendship with the world [or, we might say, going along with the performative program]," he says, "is enmity with God" (4:4). Sharing the same performative value system as the world makes it impossible to experience a fruitful and vibrant life with God, or even friendship with him.

One time when I taught through this passage, a gentleman approached me afterward to say that passages like these make God sound like an emotionally insecure person: "You can't be friends with me if you're going to be friends with *them!*" But

James is not talking about some either-or emotional immaturity of God. He's describing the nature of the human heart.

When James uses the language of "world," he's not talking about the places and the people in it. In fact, when the Bible talks about those aspects of the world, it's clear that God relates to it in love, not enmity. "For God *so loved the world*" (John 3:16, emphasis mine). But when James uses the word *world* here, he is not talking about "those out there." Rather, he is talking about the systems and values people participate in to get ahead, to feel loved, to experience glory, to satisfy desires, to be a part of something, to be seen as great, and to keep from turning into a nobody.

Today, the world is performative. The land is tilted and the paths are greased toward that way of life. And James tells us that participating in the systems and values of this world and then trying to have a life with God doesn't work. There is a conflict between the two—a conflict that often lives inside us, even if we don't realize it. Maturity and growth mean untangling that tension to begin walking more deeply with Christ.

Jesus teaches us about the deep potency of a hidden life by using the imagery of seeds. He tells two parables concerning the small mustard seed. The first is in Matthew 13:

> He put another parable before them, saying, "The kingdom of heaven is like a grain of mustard seed that a man took and sowed in his field. It is the smallest of all seeds, but when it has grown it is larger than all the garden plants and becomes a tree, so that the birds of the air come and make nests in its branches." (Matthew 13:31–32)

The second is in Matthew 17:

[Jesus said,] "For truly, I say to you, if you have faith like a grain of mustard seed, you will say to this mountain, 'Move from here to there,' and it will move, and nothing will be impossible for you." (Matthew 17:20)

These kingdom realities, however, don't begin at level 10. There is a small, hidden nature to their beginnings. A mustard seed is a common rabbinical image for small things.[2] More than that, it represents insignificance. In other words, it wasn't a positive image in their eyes. Jesus was being provocative, maybe even blasphemous, in the eyes of some of his listeners. The kingdom of God—small? And think about what happens to a tiny seed; it's buried in the ground and becomes nearly impossible to find.

That gets to Jesus' main point. He wasn't emphasizing how big the kingdom can get, since everyone in first-century Judaism knew that the kingdom of God was vast and glorious, but that it's often experienced and seen in the world in small and hidden ways, even insignificant ways by worldly standards.

Now notice that in Matthew 17, Jesus uses the same image of the mustard seed for understanding the power of our faith. There is a mustard seed dynamic to both our faith and God's kingdom. Our participation in God's kingdom must match the nature of the kingdom itself.

The performative heart is in conflict with this mustard seed dynamic. True spiritual life comes only in small measures— hidden prayer, communion with God, acts of love removed from showing off and trying to be seen. The kingdom comes into the world and into our experience not fully bloomed or with overwhelming force. This is why our faith must match the kingdom dynamic of "small to big." No one starts as a deep-rooted oak tree. We begin as seeds.

To be clear, Jesus isn't saying the kingdom and our faith grow from small hidden things to great attention-grabbing things. The growth and greatness describe the deep and wide impact they have on those who encounter them. The mustard seed dynamic is an organic process, and the power it displays becomes more and more undeniable.

Consider the life of Jesus. Most of his life was hidden, small, and isolated. He came from Nazareth, which we would call "the sticks." He was like a root from dry ground (Isaiah 53:2). And his ministry didn't start with a thunderclap. John 2 tells us that the only people who saw his first miraculous sign—turning water into wine at a wedding party—were servants, the nobodies. The most important people who could make something of the miracle didn't even know who did it. That was his calling card. He began his work with those who were supposed to be invisible at the party.

Soon afterward, in John 4, Jesus identified himself as the Messiah for the first time. But it wasn't in front of the religious or political leaders of the day; it was to a Samaritan woman who was a religious and social outcast.

Jesus launches his ministry, sharing his identity and power with social nobodies. If you were his agent, you would tell Jesus to perform his wine trick before kings and influencers. Wow the people! But instead, Jesus starts in hidden places with forgettable people, intentionally steering away from crowd-pleasers.

This was part of the reason Jesus told these mustard seed parables, to help explain why he wasn't trying to grab the biggest platforms. Nevertheless, Jesus' life and influence went from unnoticed to unignorable. This was the witness that the kingdom of God and the influence of Christ weren't hype; they weren't human influence or propaganda, but the true presence and power of God. This is how the kingdom works and how we participate in it. It's like the mustard seed that doesn't grab—it grows.

Change, Maturity, and Advancement

The New Testament has a term for this kind of growth— *maturity*. Maturity is the subtle, long-term plan for the way the kingdom of God works in us and through us and our participation in it. It's the slow path of growing out of the performative life into a life of imitating Christ. It's how we change. *Change*, however, can be a misleading word. We all want to change. We long to be different. We don't like what we are prone to do or the behavioral impulses we display. *How do I change?* is a good question, but it might be insufficient.

Instead, the New Testament gives us a vision of maturity. Of course, maturity isn't experienced apart from the dynamics of change or transformation. But we often think about change as a particular behavior that stops or starts, as if a slight modification in our life will simply wipe out the sin or addiction that's been bugging us so we can just go on with our lives. Downloading an internet filter to keep us from viewing pornography is not the same as developing sexual wholeness and maturity into the likeness of Christ with regard to our desires. Simply removing or curbing troubling behavior does not do justice to what Christ wants to do within us.

The New Testament is less concerned about behavioral modification than it is about maturity—about growing up in Christ. We are to "grow up in every way into him who is the head, into Christ" (Ephesians 4:15); we ought to grow out of being spiritual infants and "grow up into salvation" (1 Peter 2:2) and "grow in the grace and knowledge of our Lord and Savior Jesus Christ" (2 Peter 3:18). Paul's ministry was centered around presenting "everyone mature in Christ" (Colossians 1:28), calling us to "attain to the unity of the faith and of the knowledge of the Son of God, to mature manhood, to the measure of the stature of the fullness of Christ" (Ephesians 4:13). As we grow up in Christ, Paul instructs us to put aside childish things and put on maturity (1 Corinthians 13:11).

The image of maturity, a "seed to tree" dynamic, points to a mysterious and slow process. It's not simply your taking control of your life. You can't become "mature," at least not in the way the New Testament imagines it, just by deciding to become mature, any more than a seed can decide to become a tree. To become a mature, fruitful person, you must enter into the mysterious process of growing up in Christ.

Trees don't bear fruit apart from growing up into maturity. Yet the way we often pursue fruitfulness is by taping on fruit rather than producing it out of the depth of our life with Christ. Parents are often aware and convinced that they need to spend more time with their children rather than their own interests of work, entertainment, or escapism (social media or television). And there may be quick bursts of devotion toward reading and playing and shepherding their kids. But without the deep work of developing and maturing their love and dying to self, their devotion is often short-lived.

When we are convinced of our need for change, it will most often mean we need to do work in the subterranean parts of our hearts that outward behavior simply doesn't reach. Achieving change often demands the work of the spiritual disciplines of prayer and fasting and other hidden moments when Christ can expose, heal, and mature where needed. So, yes, work to give more of your presence and sacrificial time to your children if you are a parent, but be sure to mesh it with the deep work of maturity. Aim at maturity, and you get change thrown in. Aim simply at change, and you'll likely get neither.

This kind of maturity, however, is in conflict with a performative world. Our culture thinks more about *advancement* than maturity. We are more concerned with getting ahead and moving forward. Maturity doesn't pay off as quickly. Our performative culture has fooled us into thinking that advancement and accomplishment equate to maturity. Yet with all our accomplishments and advancements, we still cannot manage conflict or negotiate difficult emotions or relationships, and often our leadership positions have outpaced our maturity so we aren't able to steward them well. Consider the public stories of the downfall of spiritual leaders whose charisma and outward gifts have elevated them to high places of leadership without the depth of maturity and spiritual resources these leadership positions demand.

Alain de Botton, an agnostic philosopher, writes about how our culture has become more concerned with technological education and advancement rather than maturity in virtue:

> What is distinctive is just how selective we are about the topics we deem it possible to educate ourselves *in*. Our energies are

overwhelmingly directed toward material, scientific, and technical subjects and away from psychological and emotional ones. Much anxiety surrounds the question of how good the next generation will be at math; very little around their abilities at marriage or kindness. We devote inordinate hours to learning about tectonic plates and cloud formations, and relatively few fathoming shame and rage . . . We have the technology of an advanced civilization balancing precariously on an emotional base that has not developed much since we dwelt in caves.[3]

De Botton recognizes that we have been formed in an advancement-driven age that gives us a sense that we've matured or experienced enlightenment. Yet while we have graduate-level technological capacities, we have kindergarten-level hearts and virtue. Our culture shows its advancement through accomplishments, while the Bible calls us to a secret and hidden maturity that grows like the kingdom—like a mustard seed. It grows instead of grabs.

To follow Jesus means to abandon this way of being in the world and to begin living in a way that will likely feel out of sync with the culture around us. Listen to the words of James from the New Testament about our relationship with the world. He tells us not to go along with its systems and plans. To abandon them. Annie Dillard, in her book *Teaching a Stone to Talk*, writes this:

> God does not demand that we give up our personal dignity . . .
> God needs nothing, asks nothing, and demands nothing, like
> the stars. It is a life with God which demands these things.
> Experience has taught the race that if knowledge of God

is the end, then these habits of life are not the means but the condition in which the means operates. You do not have to do these things; not at all. God does not, I regret to report, give a hoot. You do not have to do these things—unless you want to know God. They work on you, not on him.

You do not have to sit outside in the dark. If, however, you want to look at the stars, you will find that darkness is necessary. But the stars neither require nor demand it.[4]

I don't believe God is as indifferent as Dillard makes him out to be, but you get the idea. We're to abandon the systems of the world and more intentionally enter into the "conditions" of participating in the hidden growth and maturity of the kingdom. But how do we do this?

Don't Bet on Babylon

In Matthew 13:32, Jesus gives us some direction. After comparing the kingdom of God to a mustard seed, he then says that "when it has grown it is larger than all the garden plants and becomes a tree, so that the birds of the air come and make nests in its branches." Jesus uses imagery of the kingdom as a place of rest and a center of joy. More explicitly, the kingdom of God, though it has subtle and small beginnings and its power works in contrast to the systems of this world, grows into a place of rest for the whole world. The nations will be drawn to it.

Jesus is borrowing this language from Daniel 4, where the king of Babylon, Nebuchadnezzar, had a vision of *his* kingdom being like a tree that grew strong, with limbs that reached to the clouds so all of the kingdoms of the world would see it: "Its leaves were beautiful and its fruit abundant, and in it was food for all. The beasts of the field found shade under it, and the birds of the heavens lived in its branches, and all flesh was fed from it" (Daniel 4:12).

The boast of Babylon was that it would be great and all the nations would rest on its branches. It would be the most relevant and lasting kingdom. And it *was* great. But its greatness was short-lived. A far greater kingdom was coming.

By the time Jesus spoke the parable of the mustard seed, Babylon was history. Its greatness had disappeared. It was once a powerhouse nation, but it had been surpassed by another and then another. Assyria, Babylon, Persia, Greece, and Rome all came into power successively, but none of these nations continue to this day in anything resembling their ancient forms. But Babylon continues to stick around in the New Testament imagination as a representative of worldly systems. Don't invest in Babylon, Jesus says. Its greatness is short-lived. Participate in the kingdom of God.

Even now, we sense the frailty of what at one point seemed like a dominating Western world. As modern people, we have experienced technological advancements and freedoms like no other age. At the drop of a hat (and with enough money), we're able to fly to anywhere in the world. Whatever we want, we can click "Buy Now" on Amazon for next-day delivery. My grandparents and great-grandparents were all Midwestern farmers and had to wait until certain fruits like strawberries or raspberries were in season to pick them, but now I can have them delivered on Instacart this afternoon. More than ever, we experience a kind of freedom and capacity—a hyperindividualism—to do what we want, when we want. And many of us have built our inner lives around this capacity and freedom.

But at the beginning of 2020, one little bug was released into the system—a virus—and a whole society shut down. Entire industries disappeared or went dormant. Shipping and flights became limited and expensive, if offered at all.

Did you ever imagine the world to be this fragile? At the time of the writing of this chapter, our church services have begun to see the removal of our masks during worship here in New York City. Travel has opened up more cautiously, but there is anxiety about what lies ahead. I don't know what the world will be like when you read this. But this season has shown that people who cannot imagine a life without the ability to do what they want, when they want, are spiritually fragile. Our confidence in the modern world is built on a fantasy. It provides massive amounts of wealth but no resilience—in systems or in people.

Thomas Merton describes this fantasy as a desire for "relative omnipotence":

> We are not, of course, foolish enough to imagine that we ought to find in ourselves the absolute omnipotence of God. Yet in our desire to be "as gods"—a lasting deformity impressed in our nature by original sin—we seek what one might call a "relative omnipotence": the power to have everything we want, to enjoy everything we desire, to demand that all our wishes be satisfied and that our will should never be frustrated or opposed . . . This claim to omnipotence, our deepest secret and our inmost shame, is in fact the source of all our sorrows, all our unhappiness, all our dissatisfactions, all our mistakes and deceptions. It is a radical falsity.[5]

Our world has built systems around the desire for relative omnipotence. And if we fail to live up to it (which, of course, we all do), we perform in a way that gives the impression that maybe we have lived up to relative omnipotence. The question Matthew 13 asks us is, how much have we tried to participate in this worldly kingdom? How much have we attempted to perform our way into giving others the impression that we, too, are successful in this world?

Researchers have been studying a phenomenon they call "perfectionist presentation." In this context, the term *perfectionist* is not describing someone who can't finish a task because it's never quite perfect, but rather someone who feels the need to present their life in such a way that they experience approval and belonging. British author and journalist Will Storr quotes psychology professor Gordon Flett, who describes perfectionist presentation as "the tendency to put on a false front of seeming perfect, where you cover up mistakes and shortcomings. You'll see this especially among younger people, who portray their lives on social media. For the person who feels they need to keep up with others, that seems to be an added pressure. It's like, 'Here's my perfect life, take a look at it.'"[6]

This socially pressured perfectionism, researchers say, has a strong link to suicide and self-harm. In Britain, the number of adults reporting self-harm more than doubled between 2000 and 2014.[7] Many studies show that the rise and intensification of this phenomenon came with the arrival of social media. For example, eating disorders and body dysmorphia in the US and the UK have risen by about 30 percent over that same period of time.[8] The same study shows that more than 51 percent of young adults felt more "overwhelmed" in 2016 than they did in 2009, along with increases in stress and anxiety. Depression rose by 95 percent.[9] Our performative perfectionist culture has created in us an "endless loop of self-defeating over-striving in which each new task is another opportunity for harsh self-rebuke."[10]

We are becoming increasingly fragile because we are banking our lives on a kingdom built on a fantasy that will not last. Jesus wants us to plant our hearts in different soil. Don't bet on Babylon.

Chaff That the Wind Drives Away

It's worth pausing for a moment to consider how you have participated in this performative kingdom—not to feel guilt, but to grasp how you have been shaped and what impulses have been formed in you. Jesus wants to lead us toward a good life. A life of real power and potency. Our culture has led us toward a false sense of those things. You might think of them as the "chaff" described in Psalm 1.

Those who root themselves with God and in his Word bear fruit like a tree planted by streams of water that prospers like an evergreen and is always fruitful. But those who don't, wither. They are like "chaff that the wind drives away" (Psalm 1:4). They are like a fragile shell with no resilience against the wind. Instead, Jesus wants us to flourish and "bear fruit" even into old age (Psalm 92:14).

As I mentioned earlier, Jesus gives in Matthew 17 more detail about what it means to participate in this mustard seed kingdom—mainly, that you must have mustard seed faith. The passage is set within the context of a story about a father who had come to Jesus' disciples for healing of the man's son. The son had been controlled by a demon that caused seizures that threw him into water or fire. The disciples were unable to heal the son.

Luke's gospel gives a bit more insight into what's happening in this scene. The story comes right after the disciples had been sent out on their first mission (Luke 9:1–6), followed by another mission at the beginning of Luke 10, both of which had been incredibly successful. The gospel was preached, and people everywhere were healed. The disciples explained to Jesus that even the demons were subject to them (Luke 10:17). Jesus even claimed to see Satan "fall like lightning from heaven" (v. 18).

But the demon they encountered in Matthew 17 was too much for the disciples. What happened? They had experienced a season of immense fruitfulness and success. They had power and influence. And then suddenly they met an enemy they had little power or capacity to overcome.

When the disciples asked Jesus why, he said they needed faith "like a grain of mustard seed" (Matthew 17:20). Now when Jesus describes faith like a grain of mustard seed, we immediately think size: just a little bit of faith would have been enough. And as we've already discussed, that's certainly part of what Jesus is getting at. But at a deeper level, it may refer not only to the size of their faith but also to the object. It's possible they had begun to trust their gifts and resources instead of the power of Jesus. Their greatness, success, and status defined their faith rather than Christ and his kingdom.

Previously confident, they were now bewildered by their failure. It surprised them. They seemed to believe they had everything they needed to drive out this demon, and more. You could say they had faith the size of mountains, but the object of that faith was *themselves*. Their faith was beginning to follow the methods and strategies of Babylon, not the kingdom. Jesus was correcting them by saying, in effect, "Just have a mustard seed–sized faith *in me*."

We ought to pay close attention to this dynamic in our Western culture, which has, on the whole, experienced a lot of success. Even if we personally don't feel like a success story, we are surrounded by testimonials and bestselling books about how someone got ahead or overcame difficulties by their grit, skills, gifts, resources, or education.

I pastor in Manhattan, an island that attracts highly resourced and skilled people. I am constantly surrounded by people who haven't experienced many closed doors—until suddenly, out of nowhere, they do. Movies and TV shows don't show much fragility in New Yorkers, but pastors and therapists are witnesses to it. Like the disciples in the Gospels who were surprised at what squashed their success and shook their sense of self, people who have shaped their lives around their own resources, skill sets, and inner power eventually face demons that stop them cold. Loss, suffering, relational conflict, financial ruin, or a global pandemic leave even the most confident people helpless.

Like the disciples, they ask, "Why could we not cast it out?"

For Christians, the path to answering that question is to confront the reality of where our faith is rooted. Sell your shares in the Babylonian stock. Exchange your worldly currency for a kingdom reward. The New Testament tells us we have to then resolve to live as exiles in this Babylonian world with different values and hopes that aren't celebrated, rewarded, or supported here. It's costly. But it's worth it.

Faith, Prayer, and Fasting

Mark's gospel continues the story. Jesus, after encouraging the disciples toward the mustard seed kingdom, says that demons like this "can come out by nothing but prayer and fasting" (Mark 9:29 NKJV).[11] Isn't it remarkable that faith, prayer, and fasting are the things we need when times get tough and out of our capacity to control? Jesus doesn't give techniques or tips on how to get the job done. He doesn't give a step-by-step TED Talk on how to cast out really big demons. Instead, he instructs his followers on how to get humble enough, low enough, and hidden enough.

Prayer and fasting are not methods of power and skill. If we follow Jesus' directions in Matthew 6, they are hidden, not performative. Jesus tells us to reach for neediness and longing—habits that bear witness to the fact that we have nothing sufficient within. Only Christ is sufficient. They are the spiritual practices of people who have come to the end of themselves.

When life is overwhelming, we pray and fast. We reach for mustard seed kingdom dynamics and press into hidden practices—disciplines that are unseen and ignored by the Babylonian world in which we live. But these practices align with the kingdom of God. Jesus wants us to see the potency of this hiddenness and trust it. Even when you are tempted to reach for other powers (maybe political strength or cultural clout), bury yourself, like a seed, in prayer and fasting.

Chapter 3

FRUITFUL
DORMANCY

S tudies show that young adults are increasingly placing higher expectation on others, standards that are unrealistic and overly demanding.[1] You might see this in the expectations placed on the physical attractiveness of others, whether your significant other or spouse or someone you follow on Instagram. You also might see this dynamic in the expressed demands that others have similar views on social issues and be perfect in the way they articulate these views. If someone doesn't live up to the standards we've set for them, we might body-shame them for physical imperfections in the comments of an Instagram post or cancel them on Twitter for political views we think are unacceptable in today's world. College students in particular have seen increases in "narcissism, assertiveness, and dismissive attachment" from previous generations.[2]

We might conclude that people have become more opinionated or have increasingly high standards, but that's not necessarily the case. These things are a fruit of "a preoccupation with the *perception* and *expression* of self-esteem in contemporary culture."[3] In her book *Generation Me: Why Today's Young Americans Are More Confident, Assertive, Entitled—and More Miserable Than Ever Before*, Jean Twenge, professor of psychology at San Diego State University, shows that high self-esteem has become one of the dominant development outcomes within education and parenting practices.[4] In other words, since early childhood, adults have been shaped by the expectation that they should be confident in all aspects of life. I must be confident in my body, my social and political opinions, my sexuality, my identity, my career, my income, my social status, my friendships, my marriage, and my parenting. To lack confidence in these areas is seen as a failure of either personal or moral development.

Young people report that "their social context is increasingly demanding, that others judge them harshly," because these things are demonstrably true.[5] They feel increased pressure to have their lives together so they can feel confident in themselves. And the easiest way to express confidence in yourself and show others you have your life together is to attack and shame those who evidently don't.

A woman in our church told me, "It's not that my parents simply had high expectations for me, but that they expected me to have high expectations for myself. That I could do anything and accomplish any goal I set my mind to. The problem is, when I fail, I have to give the impression to others that I didn't fail, or I feel the pressure to spin my failure as just one of the steps toward greatness." We have to present ourselves as confident in our opinions, plans, and identity, proving our high self-esteem. Our impulse, then, is to carefully curate our public image—to the extent that people often look back at the image they previously presented of themselves online and don't even recognize that person.

A few years back, I sat with an older gentleman at his retirement party. I was surprised by his unique and unmistakable happiness. Everyone knew him for this. His face was gentle, and his demeanor with others was gracious. The story of his career included a few significant failures and didn't end with what we would normally recognize as success. At one point, he was a pastor and church planter, but his pastoral ministry was difficult, and he felt unable to do the job well. So he shifted careers midway through his life, which carried with it all kinds of setbacks. He experienced long seasons of what you might call *dormancy*—he wasn't actively achieving anything most would identify as success. But here he was at seventy-two years old, with friends from all over the United States celebrating his life—a life that had significant impact on many pastors and spiritual leaders, both young and old.

As I sat with him as the party was ending, he was telling stories of friends and churches he had known or supported along the way. I asked him what helped him persevere through the years. He answered, "I think the Lord helped me learn how to welcome the parts of me that were mediocre. To reach spiritual maturity, I think it's more important than we realize to be okay with our mediocre selves and trust in God's love."

Try to grasp that contrast. Most of us have internalized the idea that "mediocre" is akin to a lack of a fully developed self. It's a lack of something unique or special. We hide what is mediocre with filters, or at least we try to. But here was a gentleman who understood that part of the substance of being a fully developed self is a willingness to welcome the mediocre aspects of life. He was a child of God and could just be himself and be loved.

Dying to Self

As mentioned in previous chapters, part of grasping and growing in the direction of a fully developed self means we intentionally and consciously resist how our culture has shaped us into performative selves. In the Gospels, Jesus has been providing a path for us in this way. So far, he has taught us to live our lives in a secret way with the Father (see chapter 1) and follow the pattern of a mustard seed kingdom (see chapter 2). Our culture perpetuates the idea that our self-worth comes from being who others think we ought to be, leading to performance-driven lives that are exhausting and dissatisfying. But Jesus leads us to paths of renewal, in which we find a deeper life with the Father and trust in the patterns of the kingdom of God rather than Babylon. In John 12, Jesus continues to describe this path that resists the performative ways of the world.

John 12 marks a critical point in the public ministry of Jesus. Often in the narrative of some successful business or personal triumph, we see a critical turning point where things can go badly or where victory is secured. Think of the time when Apple made Steve Jobs CEO in 2000 after firing him in 1985, or when Winston Churchill visited Germany in the 1930s and saw the evil of Nazism for himself. These moments secured a particular trajectory in the narrative.

This scene in John 12 is a similar moment. You might say this is the height of the "Jesus movement." His fame had spread throughout Jerusalem and Judea. He had frustrated the status quo of the religious communities. His teachings were authoritative in ways people hadn't seen before. His signs and miracles had moved him to an unignorable status.

Now the nations were coming to Jesus. In John 12:20, Greeks were looking for him. They were wanting to see and know him. The Old Testament had foreshadowed that the Gentiles would come to Jerusalem and worship the Lord in his temple (see Isaiah 2:2), and here we see hints of that reality. Jesus' reputation was spreading. People were ready to follow him. Earlier in the gospel of John, the crowds had already tried to make Jesus king (John 6:15). What would he do now? Was this how the kingdom would advance? Through bigger and better platforms? Would Jesus make the jump from local to global influencer?

Surprisingly, he resists this move. In fact, he does the opposite. The Son will still be glorified, but not through the path we might expect. He didn't follow a straight path from his growing influence to God's glory and the world's salvation. Instead, Jesus took an indirect route, away from the growth of his reputation to the death of it. He says, "Truly, truly, I say to you, unless a grain of wheat falls into the earth and dies, it remains alone; but if it dies, it bears much fruit" (John 12:24).

Here, Jesus is talking about *his own path*. Instead of taking a path to greater heights of recognition, he uses the imagery of a seed dying in the ground to explain his direction in life—to death. The way of salvation and the blessing of the whole world were not through his upward growth trajectory toward power or his surging ability to impact the world, but through humiliation, rejection, and death. Salvation and glorification come through Jesus' dying to fame, dying to power, and dying to life itself.

And that's the pattern we are called to follow as well: "Whoever loves his life loses it, and whoever hates his life in this world will keep it for eternal life. If anyone serves me, he must follow me" (John 12:25–26). Jesus is describing what Paul calls "dying to self" (see Galatians 2:20; Colossians 3:3–5). It's a life in contrast with the performative life that is lived by those who anxiously seek to be seen as confident, together, balanced, and on their way to success and love; those who seek to find a sense of self-worth and identity through the curation of a public image.

But Jesus calls us to find our self by being buried with him, like a seed, dormant in the ground.

As we saw in chapter 2, the path Jesus lays for us contradicts the paths that the worldly "Babylonian" kingdom points us toward. Jesus shows how fragile that kingdom really is. Yet we often impulsively trust what Babylon promises us. Babylon makes two kinds of promises—maximum control and maximum freedom.

With *maximum control*, I am in complete control of my destiny. I form my identity and justify my existence, needing no one else to define or shape my life. I belong to myself.

Maximum freedom is a newer development. In previous societies, people identified themselves as citizens and neighbors. But now we are primarily consumers and spectators, afraid of commitment, worrying that making commitments will reduce our freedom and cut us off from the myriad choices that constantly entice us.[6]

Our modern world bombards us with institutions, social media, and the advertisement of commodities that reinforce these promises. But the kingdoms of the world and their promises are frail. We've seen how COVID-19 shut the whole thing down in a snap and exposed how fragile these promises are. Some of us used the stimulus checks distributed by the government for financial relief in the United States to try to duct-tape these promises together, holding on to them for as long as we could. But Jesus warns that those who want to hold on to this life will lose it. As the promises of maximum control and maximum freedom are exposed as tenuous, we can either die to the kingdoms of this world, letting go of their promises with Jesus, or double down on them and become weaker, more fragile people.

Uncreated Fullness

When the plague hit London in the seventeenth century, the English minister Samuel Shaw's family was hit hard. He and his wife both fell ill. Although they recovered, they lost two children. Shaw ministered to and buried countless people in London. He wrote as a first-person witness to the plague's impact, both physical and spiritual.[7] He wrote that times of trouble are an opportunity to reflect on and give witness to what he calls the "created fullness" and the "uncreated fullness." In times of loss, we experience the frailty of the created fullness (fullness that we try to find in our things, money, health, success, or status): "Poverty empties your money; sickness empties your health; old age empties your potential; suffering empties your sense of well-being."[8]

Once you are disenchanted with the created fullness, you can embrace uncreated fullness:

> Then is a soul raised to its just altitude, to the very height of its being, when it can spend all its powers upon the supreme and self-sufficient good, spreading and stretching itself upon God with full contentment, and wrapping up itself entirely in him. This is the soul's way of living above losses; and he that so lives, though he may often be a loser, yet shall never be at a loss. He who feeds upon created goodness or sweetness, may soon eat himself out of all; the stock will be spent, and which is worse, the soul will be dried up that hath nothing else to nourish it. But he who lives upon uncreated fullness, is never at a loss, though he lose never so much of the creature: for who will value the spilling of a dish of water, who hath a well of living water at his door.[9]

Jesus shows us two kinds of lives—one that goes along with the systems and promises of a performative Babylonian world and another that patterns itself after a mustard seed kingdom, with hidden practices performed in secret with the Father. The difference between the two isn't subtle. One lives on created goodness, the other on uncreated goodness. Only one can "live above the losses."

The way from a performative life to a life hidden in Christ is death. And it feels like death too. Walking away from a performative life isn't a snap decision. As we talked about in chapter 1, it's a life of small crucifying steps. A performative life means you have reached for certain gratifying means to give you a sense of self. To resist this path will expose how dependent you have been on those measures. It's certainly easier to strive after things like dressing your kids up in trendy clothes and posing them in your beautiful kitchen while they watch you cook on top of a large island with tung oil–stained wood countertops under the stainless-steel range hood, laughing at all the clever things you say to them, making everyone wish they had your life.

It may be expensive to perform this act, but it's easier than doing the hard relational work of family life. And if you don't have the money, then the internet will send you ads from tailored algorithms for all the things you will need to manufacture this scenario. In our culture, the performance of the self is more important than the reality, and the market is happy to assist us in that way.

To follow Christ into this death, however, doesn't just mean you may miss out on the adoration in the Instagram comments. You will likely get overlooked, ignored, or dismissed. Popular culture puts forth the narrative that if you stop trying to *prove* yourself to the world, you'll *show* the world that they can't ignore you. How many books and movies are based on the narrative of the hero trying to live under the radar but inevitably becoming a beloved celebrity? While Harry Potter tries not to be noticed, the world can't resist making him a hero. Or consider how Thomas Anderson in *The Matrix*, who has no interest in being sucked into leading the rebellion against the machines, becomes The One, beloved by thousands of people who have never even met him.

But the world often ignores those who don't participate in the systems of performance—and not in a "stay dormant until the world recognizes your importance" kind of way. Going from a performative life to a hidden one with Christ can be lonely, confusing, and disorienting. It can be heartbreaking to discover how many of your relationships were transactional at work, online, and even at church when you begin, more and more, to break away from a life of performance.

And while you may be reaching for more hidden ways of living, the world isn't and won't. That can be costly and alienating. Alan Noble, in his book *You Are Not Your Own*, explains that the world will carry on as is, prioritizing visual indicators of success and telling you that you need to as well: "Almost every institution will treat you like an autonomous individual, subject to instrumentalization and valued according to efficiency . . . Instagram will not suddenly disappear when you realize you belong to Christ. There is no magic here, only a confused, desperate, anxious world, and God. There is only technique, dehumanization, self-medication, and Christ's love. There is only the freedom to accept the truth about your existence, even when it doesn't change the world or fix all your problems."[10]

Choosing to follow Christ into the ground, buried like a seed, resisting the performative life, will likely make you seem strange. You will feel out of sync at times. This will feel like death. But in many places in the Gospels, Jesus tells us up front that it will be this way (Matthew 10:38; 16:24; 24:9; Mark 8:34; Luke 9:23; 14:27; see also Paul's teaching in Philippians 1:29; 1 Thessalonians 3:3; 2 Timothy 3:12). To follow Jesus is to follow in the pattern of his life—a cruciform life. He tells us to pick up our cross and follow him. Jesus wasn't underselling the Christian life so we would be happy when we discover it isn't as bad as Jesus said it would be. No, he was being clear so we would be able to count the cost ahead of time.

When we begin to walk with Jesus, resisting the performative life, it is definitely costly, but it's worth it. In the last chapter, we reflected on the process of maturity, which is surely an important dynamic for those of us who are feeling the cost. As we meditate on Jesus' uncreated goodness, we will mature—not quickly, but surely. And as we mature, the deathly losses do not happen less frequently, but they do become more appropriately weighted. The sufficiency of created goodness will run out in these painful times, but Christ's sufficiency will not. We will begin to say with the apostle Paul:

> So we do not lose heart. Though our outer self is wasting away, our inner self is being renewed day by day. For this light momentary affliction is preparing for us an eternal weight of glory beyond all comparison, as we look not to the things that are seen but to the things that are unseen. For the things that are seen are transient, but the things that are unseen are eternal. (2 Corinthians 4:16–18)

This is the soul's way of living above the losses. As we mature, our losses begin to feel more and more weightless *in comparison* to the weight of glory that we already experience in Christ and what is being prepared for us in the future.

A Buried Life

Jesus' imagery of a buried seed gives us still more to grasp. He shows a kind of life that leads to death and a kind of death that leads to life. And perhaps unsurprisingly, the death that leads to life involves a burial. Jesus compares his life to what happens to a seed: he died and then was *buried*. When a seed is buried in the ground, it looks dead and dormant. But, of course, the dormancy is fruitful. If you didn't know what the seed was supposed to do, you'd think that burying it in the ground was the end of the story. But the seed actually becomes what it was meant to be—a great tree that bears much fruit. But if it isn't buried, it remains alone, never experiencing the end for which it was made. Jesus stepped into this kind of death, dying to the kingdoms of this world and never trusting in their promises. Literally and figuratively, he was buried in the ground. Dead and still.

Jesus presents this pattern of death and burial to us as a way of life. In the eyes of the world, a person resisting performance has just given up. It's the end of the story. A buried life. But that's only because the world does not understand what our life is for. For Christians, the New Testament says we are buried, or hidden, in and with Christ. Paul writes, "For you have died, and your life is hidden with Christ in God" (Colossians 3:3). And in Romans 6:4, Paul writes, "We were buried therefore with him by baptism into death." We are buried, not in some indifferent earth, but in Christ. It's a death, but it's not *only* a death; it's a fruitful dormancy. While our culture teaches us to find our identity in self-expression and displayed virtue, Christ leads us to find ourselves buried with him.

A life buried in Christ becomes what it was meant to be. Like a seed created for soil, we are meant to be in Christ. Apart from this kind of death, we remain alone, unsatisfied, unfruitful—living in ways we were not meant to live. In Christ, we have a *received identity* rather than a curated one that requires consistent upkeep, improvements, and filters. We were meant to live under the loving gaze of God and his acknowledgment of us rather than trying to display a life that measures up to the world's standard for a balanced, optimized, or admirable life. While we crave the "I want your life!" Instagram comments, what we need is the consistent voice of the Father telling us, "You are my beloved. Well done. I love you." We were created to live on the Father's affirmation in Christ. The affirmation of the world is a moving target, leaving us perpetually anxious and cultivating our insecurities, but the Father's voice of love is stable and firm, forming us into resilient people.

When you are buried with Christ, I don't mean you go into hiding; it's just that the world overlooks you. You are not playing the game—displaying your success, giving evidence of your right opinions, and curating your exceptional life of leisure, travel, intelligence, and virtue. If you do, you will be like the seed that never goes into the ground. It is left alone.

A deep loneliness comes for those who live off a curated image. It's heartbreaking. We can have many followers but few friends, lots of comments but no communion. A 2020 study from

Harvard University shows that 61 percent of those from ages eighteen to twenty-five reported feeling lonely "frequently" or "almost all the time or all the time."[11] Even more, "the unsettling statistic is even more troubling when combined with June [2020] data from the Centers for Disease Control and Prevention showing that 63 percent of young people reported experiencing substantial symptoms of anxiety and depression."[12]

But when you're buried, the substance of your identity, meaning, and self-worth will be found not through the performance of the self but through the death and burial of the self in Christ. And in that burial is the soil and setting for fruitfulness. Because your burial is in Christ, what was available to Christ is available to you. This is why being buried with Christ is a *fruitful dormancy*. All the resources that Christ had we now have *in him*.

This is what Christians call our *union* with Christ. When Christ came in the incarnation, he took on everything that was ours so we could take on everything that was his. If you are in Christ, what is true of Christ is true of you; what belongs to Christ belongs to you. Your past, present, and future are then defined by the past, present, and future of Christ, not your failures, weaknesses, and shame. If you are buried with Jesus, your future is as bright as the glorified Christ in heaven.

There is no curation of our image when we are in Christ. You cannot add to or enhance who you are in him. In Christ, as Paul tells us in Ephesians, are all the benefits and blessings in the heavenly places (1:3).

Which brings us to a nuance that may seem like a small detail, but I promise you it isn't. There is a way of reading of John 12:23–28 that just perpetuates the worldly performative way of life. You may hear a church say something like, "Stop living for the world and live for Jesus," which sounds right, but unless we unearth the root of our performative impulse, we're just exchanging the world we are performing for with Jesus.

Is it wrong to perform for Jesus instead of the world? Yes, it absolutely is. Who we are—our identity and self-worth—is not based on what we do and provide for Christ; it's received as a gift by way of being united to him already. In other words, we must be careful not to simply replace our performative life in the world with a performative life for Christ—which is just as exhausting and demanding.

So pay close attention to this truth: When Christ calls us to a "death and burial" life rather than a performative one, the call is to die not *for* Christ but *with* Christ. This truth makes all the difference. Christ does not need our death like we needed his.

It's interesting to note that John 12 observes that Jesus and his disciples were on the way to the Passover Feast. Of course, at the cross, Jesus identified most profoundly with the sacrificial lamb. But according to the book of Leviticus, during the Feast of Firstfruits, which immediately followed the Passover, the people would give the first grain and seeds of the harvest in sacrifice and worship (Leviticus 23:9–14). Here Jesus connects himself to this image; he describes himself as a sacrificial seed—dying, breaking open, and being buried in the ground.

Interestingly, when the Greeks came and wanted to see and know Jesus, he knew the only way they truly and eternally could see and know him was for him not simply to greet them, thank them for their support, and wow them with a quick miracle, but to die for them. He would rather be friends with those Gentiles for eternity than receive momentary praise and adoration from them—truly dying to the Babylonian kingdom. That's true for us as well. Jesus died that he might have us as friends. It was an act of deep, infinite love.

And now he invites us into this pattern of life in fellowship with him—a "fellowship of His sufferings" (Philippians 3:10 NKJV). Since we die with Christ, we are buried, but we are not alone. We may be ignored and alienated by the world, but not by Jesus. Yes, Jesus calls us his servants in this passage. But the gospel of John doesn't allow the reality of being "a servant of Christ" to contradict being "a friend of Christ" (see John 15:15 [NIV]: "I no longer call you servants, because a servant does not know his master's business. Instead, I have called you friends"). We might call this *the friendship of his sufferings*.

To take it one step further, as Christ is a companion to our sufferings, something of our union with him allows us also to be a companion to his sufferings. Our experiences of loneliness and pain find a deeper sense of meaning in his experiences of loneliness and pain. As he condescends to our lives, we transcend to his. If your life is a seed, then this is the soil you were made to be buried in.

A Fruitful Life

The climax of the imagery is that the seed "bears much fruit" (John 12:24). Despite the death and burial and the cost and trouble of refusing the performative life, fruitfulness (at least the kind Jesus imagines) comes only on the other side of the dormancy with Christ. Seeds unburied never bear fruit.

If you've read this book up to this point, it's likely you long for this kind of participation in the kingdom rather than the performative world that sucks us in and incentivizes our insecurities. The costs are worth it, but they are real. The fruit, however, is real also. A life buried with Christ, dead and dormant to the Babylonian systems, has a deeper capacity for fruitful living in God's kingdom. Instead of a performance, people experience our hospitality. Instead of our opinions, they experience our generosity. Instead of our insecurities, they experience the presence of Christ.

Chapter 4

SOWING OUR DEATH

When our family moved to New York City, our church couldn't support a full-time salary yet, so for the first three years, I worked another job as well. We felt some anxiety about whether we could keep up, especially with three young kids in a small Manhattan apartment. But I had maintained a similar pace through graduate school, so I felt I could handle the challenge.

In seminary, I studied with a full load of classes, followed by a shift at the campus bookstore, and then I'd drive to a local church where I mopped floors and did other janitorial work. I'd come home for a half hour to wrestle with our two kids before Jena would hand me a sandwich as I ran out the door to load trucks at UPS at night. Homework was done in parking lots before my shifts and at other odd hours. Sweaty and exhausted, I'd come home at night, take a shower, scarf down a late dinner, and collapse into bed in order to wake up early to do it all over again.

By the time we moved to New York City, my body seemed to have stored enough muscle memory of the grind to know what was needed to keep the pace. But this new season had a key difference I didn't expect going in. Unlike my string of odd jobs during graduate school, pastoral ministry often demanded an unhurried pace. I couldn't say to someone who was grieving, "Okay, I'm going to sit with you for twenty-five minutes, and then I have to get back to sermon writing." No, I learned that I often had to sit with people in their grief or trouble, listening and praying, for as long as they needed.

In graduate school, I would cram in homework in the early mornings, late at night, on weekends, and in parking lots before my shifts started. It was crazy, but I knew I could get everything done because there were clear demarcations between when one thing started and another ended. I knew how much time I had. But as a pastor, I couldn't hustle through my work. People aren't tasks, and sermons aren't class papers. But as I mentioned above, I also had *another* job where I did editorial work that demanded my attention and care as well.

I developed a deep anxiety that I was constantly letting people down, not following through, not doing enough or being present enough. I felt guilty for taking days off. During one spring, we planned a trip to Cape Cod. It was our first family vacation. We couldn't quite afford the trip, so we Airbnbed our apartment to pay for everything. The day before we left, I woke up with terrible stomach pains. They got increasingly worse, so I went to the urgent care clinic, where they told me I had appendicitis.

After my emergency surgery, the doctors gave us instructions for my recovery—get lots of rest and don't pick up anything over five pounds! My wife looked at them and said in a clear and serious tone, "We are leaving for a trip tomorrow. We have four Swedish women flying in to stay at our apartment while we are gone. Is it okay if I just put him in the car and drive him out of town?" The doctor stared at her, blinked, and said, "Sure. Just don't let him drive or pick anything up." We had just had our fourth child. So that made me a fifth child my wife would have to take care of by herself on our road trip. And I still needed to find time to write my sermon for the coming Sunday.

By the time the church could cover my full salary and I could quit my second job, I was weary and burned-out. It took a while for my body to learn that I wasn't working two jobs. At times, as I played with my kids, I would suddenly panic and feel for my phone, trying to remember if I had gotten everything done, responded to all the emails, and returned all the calls to ensure that I let down as few people as possible. It would be a while before I felt normal again.

A World Built for Machines

We often say someone is "a machine" when they can do or produce more than what is normal. We generally mean it as a compliment. As I reflect on that especially busy season, I remember how much I felt like I needed to be a machine—and not in a positive way. I needed to be something more (or maybe less) than human. I needed to do things that ignored normal human limitations. I slept very little. I kept going when my body needed me to stop.

Jena and I adapted to a season that emptied us of a lot of energy. But we also attached to it a sense of calling and obedience. We knew that season was a means to an end, not a long-term vision of a sustainable, good life.

But since that time, I have noticed that this burnout and its accompanying weariness are features of ordinary existence for many of us—the "permanent residence" of our society.[1] In conversations with people in our church community and neighborhood, I see signs of inner fatigue that I am intimately familiar with. We're tempted to blame overwork on ungodly ambition, and that can often be the case. But we also live in a world with ungodly systems that, as L. M. Sacasas explains, demand "that human beings operate at a scale and pace that is not conducive to their well-being—let alone rest, rightly understood—but by now most of us have been born into this state of affairs and take it more or less for granted."[2] Sacasas makes the case that the "human-built world is not built for humans."

Anne Helen Petersen points out that in this "human-built world" of ours, "the ideal worker, after all, is a robot." We have arranged society to "effectively revenge rest."

> A robot never tires, never needs rest, requires only the most basic of maintenance. When or if it collapses, it is readily replicated and replaced. In *24/7: Late Capitalism and the Ends of Sleep*, Jonathan Crary makes the haunting case that we're already training our bodies for this purpose. The more capable you are of working without rest of any form—the more you can convince your body and yourself to labor as a robot—the more valuable you become within the marketplace. We don't turn off so much as go into "sleep mode": ready, like the machines we've forced our bodies to approximate, to be turned back on again.[3]

Sacasas points out that while "human beings are remarkably resilient and adaptable" and can often adapt to difficult and inhumane environments in wartime, he asks, "Is it good for human beings to adapt to the new state of affairs?"[4] Is it good for human beings to become machine-like? When we just assume this state of affairs is the status quo, we often feel guilty for not keeping up. When we feel exhausted or depleted of the energy needed to sustain ourselves in this environment, our superficial analysis tells us, *I must be the problem*. To keep up with this robotic ideal, we optimize ourselves to be as productive and efficient as possible. We watch TED Talks and listen to podcasts on how to best optimize our eating habits, relational habits, even "rest habits."[5]

With these new strategies, we can, in one week, come out swinging, confident that we have what it takes and the strategies to sustain, but in another week we feel as if we are just barely holding on. Nobody is ever as productive as we hope to be or as rested as we should be. We all seem to be floating between the extremes of optimization and self-medication.

This is, of course, the Babylonian kingdom and its systems that Jesus teaches us to resist, where we are drawn to participate in a society whose rhythms, scale, pace, and demands are not conducive to our well-being. And the remedies offered do not correct the larger destructive system. They merely optimize us to keep us functioning within the system or medicate us when we sense the limits of our capabilities.

Chapter 3 emphasized the need to die to the promises and incentives of this Babylonian kingdom. But I also understand how this can get complicated. Many folks in our church community work in industries that place inhumane expectations on their employees, but they also have families, retirement, rent, or mortgage payments that make them dependent on remaining at their jobs. I rarely advise that people leave their field of work just because the industry is toxic. It's hard to find an industry that isn't. Whether it's finance, academia, politics (local, state, or national), advertising, information technology, art, trade, publishing, media, or health care, most industries can be competitive and performative.

The option of simply quitting is rarely available to anyone. But we must engage in deep and difficult reflection on whether we *perform* for our careers. There's a difference between working in an industry and living for its promises. Jesus commands us to die to the latter. As we've learned, doing so will be costly. You will seem strange to others and alienated at times. And because industries have incentives to get you to go along with their vision of the good life, it might keep you from getting the promotions you hope for and the access you desire. It may even end up costing you your job—bringing financial trouble and steep cuts in your standard of living.

Just this week, I had a long conversation with a friend in our church community who works in publishing here in New York. Her gifts and intelligence have gotten her into great opportunities and positions. But she's also a deeply mature follower of Jesus. More and more, she has had to give up greater opportunities and places of power, since she lives for the promises of Christ, not the promises offered by her industry. For years she has had to consider and wrestle with what she has with Jesus versus what the world offers her. It has cost her greatly. Jesus tells us over and over that following him will be costly.

We shouldn't move past this truth too quickly. Take a deep breath and read this next sentence slowly: *If you remain with Christ, resisting the performative life, you will feel tension, pressure, and pain.* Jesus is clear that life with him is a cruciform life. Maybe our impulse is to simply hope that it won't happen that way. But clinging to that impulse won't serve us well. At best, it is a hope that Jesus was wrong or at least exaggerating the threat. Jesus, however, was preparing us for a deeper, more joyful life, even in the midst of trouble.

The Resurrection Life

Remember the Beatitudes of Matthew 5? Blessed are the meek, the peacekeepers, the poor in spirit. But also, "Blessed are those who are persecuted because of righteousness, for theirs is the kingdom of heaven. Blessed are you when people insult you, persecute you and falsely say all kinds of evil against you because of me" (Matthew 5:10–11 NIV). Jesus envisions this life as one not simply of loss but of blessing. We can spiritually and emotionally thrive when we are culturally and socially diminished.

Now we saw in the previous chapter that Jesus uses the imagery of a seed buried in the ground to explain how we might understand dying to the promises and incentives of the Babylonian kingdoms of the world (see John 12:20–26). Interestingly, the apostle Paul uses the same seed imagery in 1 Corinthians 15 to help us grasp this dynamic more deeply. But while Jesus emphasizes the *dying* of the seed, Paul emphasizes the *living* of it. First Corinthians 15 is all about resurrection!

A literal, physical resurrection is coming for you if you are in Christ. Christ has risen from the dead, and so will you. Paul argues that all other victories and losses must be put in perspective in light of the reality of this one great victory in Christ.

Jesus, in John 12, emphasizes what we must *die from*. Paul, in 1 Corinthians 15, stresses what we must *live to*. Jesus points to the cost, Paul to the power. But both accentuate the burial of a seed: "What you sow does not come to life unless it dies" (1 Corinthians 15:36). Here we hear echoes of what Jesus told us: "Unless a grain of wheat falls into the earth and dies, it remains alone" (John 12:24). But Paul puts an important emphasis not just on "bearing fruit," as Jesus teaches, but on experiencing resurrection power *through death*.

Here's the principle that Paul wants us to understand: Nothing comes to life unless it dies. There's a kind of power and life and joy that comes *only* through the death and decay of our previous ways of being, our previous desires and hopes. When Jesus envisions a life that spiritually and emotionally thrives, even when it is culturally and socially diminished, he reminds us that it can come only through resurrection dynamics. And the only things that can be resurrected are dead.

Isn't that striking? The death and resurrection of Jesus become a pattern of life for Christians—not just a onetime occurrence for us at the end, but a regular way of living. We experience a pattern of uprooting and dying to the kingdoms and promises of this world in order to *become alive* to something deeper. Just as our family and friends will bury our bodies in the dirt when we die—like sowing a seed—expecting Christ to transform our bodies into glory, we are also sowing our death to the promises of this world, expecting Christ to do something miraculous with it. What kind of life will he bring to our daily crucifying steps? Floating between the extremes of optimization and self-medication is a path that slowly dehumanizes us, reducing our lives to futility. That kind of death-life has no generative power. In the end, it is vanity. But Jesus and Paul are leading us to a kind of death-life that results in power, resurrection, fruitfulness, and joy.

Paul gives us two important principles for this resurrection life. He writes in 1 Corinthians 15:37, "What you sow is not the body that is to be, but a bare kernel."

Offering a Bare Kernel

First, remember that we are not the ones doing the transforming. A resurrection life, full of power and joy from the death we are sowing, is not primarily our work. We participate in the work, but we are not the source of its power. Just like in our bodily resurrection in the end, what we offer the ground as a seed is our dead body, not the gloriously resurrected one. Take note: What we offer Christ is not a transformed life, but simply *our life*.

This process has a continuity and a discontinuity to it. Like the "seed to plant" dynamic, there is a continuity to what happens to us when we die to the kingdoms and promises of the world. There is a cause and effect. We become deeper people with thicker lives, and a spiritual vitality helps us live above the losses, especially the losses that come because we have abided with Christ in this Babylonian world. What dies and is sown comes to life again.

But there is also a discontinuity. When you put a seed into the ground, it doesn't just become a bigger or better seed. It becomes something different. The death process transforms the seed into something new.

When we are bodily and physically resurrected, we are not simply becoming something we could have done ourselves if we just had a little more time or were a little more consistent with our diet and exercise habits. We will be glorified. The product of our glorification by death is radically different than what it was before, like a redwood tree is different from its seed. There is no optimizing for resurrection. It's divine intervention or bust.

Just like in our bodily resurrection, then, we bring only the "bare kernel." Christ resurrects and transforms. The only thing we offer to this dynamic is a dead body. We sow our death—death to self, death to sin, and death to the vision of a good life that calls for our performative selves.

Welcoming the Unwelcome Parts of Ourselves

This leads to a second and potentially more difficult principle: We must offer ourselves *as we truly are* to this death Christ has for us, not a selective version of ourselves, which is what we are prone to do.

So far, you may have recognized the performative parts of yourself in some of our reflections. And maybe it's a version of yourself you do not like, so your impulsive safety scheme is to deny that it exists, justify why your behavior is needed, or simply dismiss the importance of paying attention to it. But when we deny, justify, or dismiss these parts of our lives, they do not go away. They just grow deeper into the muscle memory of our lives, subconsciously driving our decisions and shaping our fears. As David Benner warns, "Powerful conditioning in childhood encourages us to acknowledge only the most acceptable parts of our self. And parts of self that are not given a place at the family table become stronger, not weaker. Operating out of sight and beyond awareness, they have increasing influence on our behavior."[6]

The difficult part of this dying that Jesus and Paul lead us in is that it is very intentional work. We cannot passively acknowledge where we have begun leading a performative life, what false promises we are placing our hope in, what safety schemes we are taking refuge in apart from Christ. We must actively resist the performative life, even when it's costly.

The resurrection power is from Christ, and only he can

transform us. As long as we hold on to our safety schemes of denying, justifying, and dismissing, we may be kept safe from having to acknowledge our shadows, but we also distance ourselves from divine healing and life.

Many of us are not comfortable bringing all the unsavory and performative parts of our lives to the surface for Christ to heal because we lack grace for ourselves. We've come to dislike who we've become, which is part of the reason we live performative lives. We don't think our neighbors will welcome our true selves, so neither do we. This is the true darkness of a performative society—self-hatred. We rarely give grace to those we hate.

Consider giving yourself some grace. Now before you write this portion off as just some positive-thinking reinforcement, please consider that Jesus welcomed sinners. He dined with prostitutes and tax collectors *before* their lives were reformed, not after. If Jesus welcomed sinners, how can you do less? We must welcome the unwelcome parts of ourselves in order to experience the power and healing of Christ.

You may read this and assume we are talking about justifying and accepting our sin. No, the New Testament is clear that we must crucify our sins (see Romans 8:13). But denying our shadows is not the same as crucifying them. Only what we are honest and open about gets crucified. As Benner puts it, "Attempts to eliminate things that we find in our self that we do not first accept as part of us rely on denial, not crucifixion."[7]

When we come to Christ in prayer, we should remember that we are not coming already transformed, but in need of transformation. Jesus is not waiting for us to transform our lives before we come to him; he's waiting for us to come to him for transformation and healing. We don't hide our wounds and weaknesses from our doctors, nor do we hide our performative lives from Christ.

Don't Steal God's Healing

As I left the room of a difficult counseling meeting with a young man in our church, another church leader who was present in the meeting beckoned me over and said, "Make sure you don't try to steal God's healing for him."

I had asked this leader to join us after several meetings with the young man had not gone well. Our times together had been difficult and confusing. The problem was not with the person I was counseling. He was suffering and simply trying to make sense of it. The problem was me.

I was still in the first few years of pastoral ministry and trying my best to care for those in my church. But this encounter exposed that I was deeply uncomfortable with other people's suffering. I had an impulse to try to take away the pain of those I was caring for and solve their struggles. I talked more than I listened, answered more questions than I asked, and gave superficial solutions to deep wounds of the heart. These pastoral care encounters had been so difficult because I was trying to do something only God could do. My colleague recognized it immediately.

Henri Nouwen, in his book *The Wounded Healer*, explains that a minister (whether a vocational pastor or just a good friend) is "not a doctor whose primary task is to take away pain," but is someone whose main role is to share in pain.[8] This was a profound discovery for me—and a difficult one. Nouwen goes on:

"When someone comes with his loneliness to the minister, he can only expect that his loneliness will be understood and felt, so that he no longer has to run away from it but can accept it."[9] I wasn't comfortable with other people's suffering because I wasn't yet fully comfortable accepting my own.

As this and previous chapters have shown, Jesus is teaching that some pains are inevitable in resisting the world and following him. Consider these pains as something to receive rather than something to resist. J. R. R. Tolkien received a letter from a priest complaining that his novels and short stories weren't theologically correct because they treated death as a gift rather than a punishment for sin after the fall. Tolkien responded, "What punishments of God are not also his gifts?"[10]

I understand if you flinch when reading that quote, but if you talk to a believer who has suffered years of pain and yet stubbornly remained joyful, truths like this, while mysterious, make existential sense. When we come to Christ, he baptizes us not only with his Spirit but also *with fire* (see Matthew 3:11). Fire, in the Bible, is not subtle. It's dramatic imagery. You put gold, silver, and precious metals into fire to remove the impurities and compromises. If you put damp wood into fire, the water comes hissing out like screams.

So it is with our hearts. We've spent years in a performative world, often unconsciously formed by its promises and seductive visions of the good life. Just as it is with gold, so we need fire to remove our compromises. God can use any kind of pain and trouble, but it's the pain of the loss we feel when resisting the world's promises and remaining with Christ that is often the most purifying. Resisting a performative life and resting in the secret places with the Father, as we've seen, often means being overlooked, ignored, alienated, pushed out, and hated. But here, in the fire, we have the growing capacity to experience the Father's voice ("I love you," "You are my beloved child," "I'm pleased with you"), his presence, and his healing.

We must see, then, the foolishness of trying to take away God's healing and replace it with our own easy fixes. We often function like false prophets with ourselves and others, claiming peace where there is none (see Jeremiah 6:14). We give superficial answers and offer false hopes. It's a bit like trying to take the impurities out of gold with our fingers. It won't work, and our fingers just add more impurities to the mix.

When the trials and troubles of walking with Christ in the Babylonian world come, receive them as gifts. Receive them as a beautifying fire and a path that leads to participation in Christ's suffering. This is a hard word, for sure. But Christ will be a faithful friend throughout. You can trust Jesus when he tells you, "Blessed are you," when you experience the pain of resisting the performative life for a secret life with the Father. As we'll see in the next chapter, God provides us with strategies for joy along the way. We can spiritually flourish, despite being culturally and socially diminished. That really is the good life.

Chapter 5

STRATEGIES
FOR JOY

Back in chapter 1, I told a bit of my own story of depression and seasons of emotional darkness. If you remember, I mentioned the temptation to perform my way out of that season rather than receiving the season as a grace and a means by which Christ was working to refine and mature me. I discovered in that season what many mothers and fathers of the faith in history discovered—that God provides strategies for joy and ways to flourish even when we are culturally and socially diminished. I mentioned my encounter with God through meditating on Psalm 81: "Open your mouth wide, and I will fill it" (v. 10). But I have been helped to see a deeper world of resources as I have tried to walk with Jesus in this world and be with others in their own troubles. This chapter aims to explain these strategies, but first we must say something about our impulse to resist them. This impulse is ancient, and Jesus has much to say about it.

An Ancient Resistance

In Matthew 16, we read how Jesus got into a boat with his disciples and warned them, "Watch and beware of the leaven of the Pharisees and Sadducees" (v. 6). The remark confused them. As they fumbled through the meaning, Jesus pointed back to their previous encounter with the Pharisees and Sadducees in which they demanded that Jesus provide a sign from heaven in order to test him (see vv. 1–4).

The religious leaders were guilty of the performative spirituality that Jesus consistently calls us to resist. They worried about the outer qualities of life more than the inner qualities, like a person washing the outside of a dish while leaving the inside (the more important part) unwashed and dirty (Matthew 23:26), or like a whitewashed tomb, which is beautified with white paint on the outside but inside holds a rotting corpse (vv. 27–28). They wanted a sign because visual markers of success (spiritual or otherwise) were the only way they knew how to evaluate someone.

Notice the imagery Jesus uses in his warning: "Watch and beware of the leaven." Leaven is the yeast in dough that causes it to rise. In the New Testament, *leaven* is used as both positive and negative imagery. Paul describes unaddressed sin in a Christian community as leaven: "A little leaven leavens the whole lump" (Galatians 5:9). Jesus, more positively, uses the imagery to describe how the kingdom of God spreads in the world, like a little bit of leaven hidden in three measures of flour "till it was all leavened" (Matthew 13:33). Both examples use leaven as imagery of a *cultural* dynamic that spreads in hidden, subtle, subversive ways—in ways that can impact and characterize us, personally and corporately, without us being fully aware. Our embracing of the cultural dynamic becomes part of the ordinary way we expect life to be.

As mentioned in previous chapters, the performative life isn't a new development, or Jesus wouldn't have had so many penetrating things to say about it. But we've looked at some modern versions of this life, where we attempt to establish an identity and a sense of self through *visual* markers and indicators of "making it." This cultural idolatry has a "leaven" nature to it. We may be surprised how deeply engrained it already is in our consciousness.

During the COVID-19 pandemic, many of us experienced loss or uncertainty about our possessions, freedoms, plans, wealth, relationships, jobs, and health. In January 2022, many people felt like we had moved on from the pandemic and were readapting to life as normal. But on the first weekend of the year, airlines canceled more than fifteen thousand flights during the height of holiday travel, mostly because airline employees called in sick with the coronavirus. We had all hoped this would be a holiday season that felt more normal, but instead it was overshadowed by the new Omicron variant.

The things we form our identity around (certain freedoms, money, relationships, jobs, and more) are fragile. We have used these things to prove to the world that we're *making it*, that we're *doing okay*. But it doesn't take something like COVID-19 to unveil this charade. Anyone who shapes their sense of self around fragile things will at some point be faced with their own fragility. That can be terribly discouraging. We become despondent, depressed, and apathetic. We lose our joy. This chapter offers spiritual direction for these times.

Weary in a Fragile World

Even after Jesus rose from the dead and commissioned his church, what is surprising is that at times we witness this "leaven" still present in the early church. Consider the scene the apostle Paul mentions in Galatians 2 that involves Peter. While Peter had eaten and fellowshiped with newly believing Gentiles, a powerful and influential group had arisen that condemned the new Gentile converts and those who associated with them because they weren't following the Mosaic law, especially the circumcision laws, in order to be spiritually included in God's people. Perhaps falling under their influence, in Galatians 2, Peter was now behaving in a way that appeased this "circumcision party." Paul had to confront Peter for performing for the circumcision party. Paul said that Peter "stood condemned" (v. 11), "acted hypocritically" (v. 13), and lived in a way that was "not in step with the truth of the gospel" (v. 14).

Not only had Peter been a part of the early church that was led by the Holy Spirit to include the Gentile converts in Christian fellowship apart from the law (see Acts 15), but he also had heard Jesus' warning years before: "Watch and beware of the leaven of the Pharisees and Sadducees" (Matthew 16:6). Peter failed to heed this warning from Jesus when faced with pressure from the circumcision party and instead allowed the cultural status quo to shape his behavior and desires.

We don't know what happened after the story of Paul confronting Peter, but we do know that Peter would have to reckon with putting his hopes in the status quo of the cultural climate. Maybe it would be the fear of losing friends among the influential or even access to certain circles of power. Worse, maybe he'd now have to wrestle with the feelings of alienation and loneliness.

If the apostle Peter had to reckon with this, then even the most spiritually mature among us will likely need to as well. Even if you grew up in a Christian environment, served on a deacon committee or elder board at church, or even served as a vocational pastor, it's best to assume the performative individualism of our age has gotten deeper into the muscle memory of your heart than you realize. And at some point, the things we knowingly or unknowingly placed our hope in or depended on to portray our success before others will crumble or disappear. In those moments, we will feel emotionally vulnerable and lost. We may be tempted toward cynicism or disillusionment. We will need stable direction on how to find joy again.

In my own moments of reckoning with this issue, Psalm 126 has been a helpful guide. It deals with disillusionment and an earnest longing for joy. This psalm is an exile song, a kind of melody the Israelites sang while feeling culturally and spiritually lost as captives in the land of Assyria or Babylon. They felt as though they had lost everything, and the story of their lives did not fit their ambitions or expectations. They were weeping.

The question that lingers in the lyrics is, how do we find joy again? Joy in the Bible is not a weak or watery concept that merely dilutes our sadness and pain. Rather it's the hard deck on which all of life finds its legs. Biblical joy is a deep reserve that remains even when everything else is collapsing. When everything else is falling apart, you aren't. A performative world can leave even the best of us weary and heavy laden. Psalm 126 aims our attention toward strategies for joy when we experience the fragility of the world around us.

Like Those Who Dream

Psalm 126 begins with a memory: "When the Lord restored the fortunes of Zion, we were like those who dream. Then our mouth was filled with laughter, and our tongue with shouts of joy" (vv. 1–2a). Even the surrounding nations were amazed: "Then they said among the nations, 'The LORD has done great things for them.' The LORD has done great things for us; we are glad" (vv. 2b–3). To persevere through these difficult circumstances, God's people remembered previous seasons of care and abundance. They practiced the ordinary rhythm of remembering: *The Lord has been so good to us.*

The phrase "we were like those who dream" sticks out to me. It reminds me of Joel 2:28, where the prophets looked forward to a time when the Spirit would be poured out on God's people, and "your old men shall dream dreams, and your young men shall see visions." It describes a season when God will be present and every prayer will be answered, when God's power will feel potent.

Both of these passages seem to be referencing a time when God spoke clearly and meaningfully through prophets to comfort his people with hope. Maybe you remember seasons like this in your own life—times when God seemed to be powerfully present. Whether or not you experienced prophetic powers is beside the point. At these times, you could look ahead to the future expectantly because God was powerfully present. You could dream.

The opposite is true when everything seems to be falling apart. In seasons of loss or grief, depression or sadness, apathy or cynicism, it's difficult to see around the corner and imagine a hopeful future. You begin to lose your ability to dream. Indifference begins to crowd into your emotional life. I mentioned in chapter 1 my own season of emotional darkness and depression that lasted about eighteen months. As the lead pastor of our church, I'm often expected to imagine what's ahead, what's coming around the corner, what to be prepared for. But I remember being in planning meetings at church and having a hard time waking up that muscle. I struggled with indifference and weariness. It was hard to dream.

I can imagine the people singing Psalm 126, remembering times when the future was eagerly awaited rather than dreaded: "We were like those who dream." They looked back on a time when they could anticipate the future and God seemed to be leading them in a hopeful direction. This isn't an act of mere nostalgia. Nostalgia is just a painkiller that numbs the discomfort for a while but doesn't heal anything. No, the type of remembering described in Psalm 126 contemplates the goodness and faithfulness of God (which are constant and true) rather than the comfort and happiness of circumstances (which are fleeting). Do you know the difference? "The LORD has done great things for us." Surely he has.

Remembering what God has done reminds us of the character of God. We remember all the graces, all the gifts, all the moments when he came through, when he lifted us up, when he provided. When Jena and I moved to New York, as I mentioned previously, we took a job at a church that couldn't quite pay a full salary. We were confident we could make it work month-to-month, but the up-front costs were daunting. In 2011, a two-bedroom apartment in Manhattan cost anywhere between $3,000 and $4,000 per month. We needed to pay our first and last month's rent, along with a security deposit (which amounted to a month's rent) and a broker fee (which was about a month's rent). That could easily add up to $12,000 to $16,000 before even stepping foot into the apartment. A month before leaving for NYC, we had to be honest and recognize we didn't have the money to even begin our first few months there.

On the last Sunday before moving, some of the leaders of the church we attended at the time brought us up onstage to pray for us. They explained to the congregation where we were going and shared some ways they could be praying for us. A few days later, as we were saying goodbye to friends over ice cream, one friend came over to us with an envelope in her hand. She mentioned that someone had been on a business trip to our town and had attended the worship service at our church on Sunday. They had prayed for us and wanted to anonymously give a financial gift to help us in our move. Grateful, I took the envelope and put it in my pocket.

When we got home, we sat down and opened it. We were stunned. God had just provided for all of our up-front costs of moving into the city. And after we moved and had gotten settled, we received another check from the same person for the same amount, covering many of our future financial needs. Both checks came at the right time. To this day, we still don't know who gave us that money.

Jena and I look back at those moments as witnesses of God's affirmation and presence in our lives. Since then, we have experienced many moments of failure, embarrassment, discouragement, weakness, and weariness. At times we have been tempted to question our calling in New York. But those instances of God's great provision are witnesses to God's calling on our lives and to our need to be faithful, despite circumstantial evidence. Jena and I can say with confidence, "The LORD has done great things for us." The practice of remembering is important because it reconfirms for us God's character and faithfulness, which run deeper than momentary and circumstantial results or success. God is good, and I can trust him and wait for him when times are hard and I'm confused.

In the first half of Psalm 126, the singers look to the past. But in the second half, they look ahead. They adopt a future-oriented anticipation that God will "restore [their] fortunes" (v. 4). When we read the Bible through the filter of this hope, we see promises assuring us that what has been lost will be restored double (Zechariah 9:12) or restored thirty, sixty, and a hundredfold (Matthew 13:8; 19:29). The prophet Joel writes of the Lord's promise to "repay you for the years the locusts have eaten" (2:25 NIV). The future hope of God's people is one of abundance in Christ.

Psalm 126 teaches us that looking at history informs our hope. Both strategies—looking to the past and looking to the future—are dependent on each other. For example, consider what Paul tells us in Romans 8:32: "He [God] who did not spare his own Son but gave him up for us all"—that's our history—"how will he not also with him graciously give us all things?"—that's our hope. A spirituality that looks only to the past is simply nostalgic or sentimental. A spirituality that looks only to the future is hype. Both ring hollow in times of pain.

The practice of remembering is a critical strategy for joy because Christianity is historical in nature, even if you don't have seemingly miraculous stories to tell. At one level, God is actively present in our life. His divine activity is not on some other plane of reality. He listens and answers prayers—*my prayers*. He comforts *my heart*. He speaks love *to me* through his Spirit. He counts how many times *I toss* at night (see Psalm 56:8). He tells me to cast *my anxieties* on him (see 1 Peter 5:7).

When I look back at my life, I witness a history of God's presence and care for me.

But on another level, the cross of Christ shows that even the greatest tragedy, the death of the incarnate Son of God, is transformed into the greatest good for God's people—our salvation. The cross is the greatest *witness* of God's historical faithfulness, proving to our hearts that our trial and trouble, darkness and loss, pain and embarrassment will not have the last word for us. Some of us may have miraculous stories of personal, dramatic divine intervention. But *all of us* have the cross.

Shame and Self-Hatred

The trouble is that often, even when we practice this remembrance and let it inform our view of the future, hope can feel distant and joy fleeting. There's a theological explanation for this: Only the Spirit of God can pour out a sense of thick hope and stable joy. So many of the psalms call believers to "wait for the LORD." About two dozen take up the theme of waiting for the Lord to act on the writer's behalf or to restore the writer's emotional life with joy. Psalm 126 is in this family of psalms. The psalmist is not merely waiting for circumstantial change or trying a mental technique to generate happiness. When we remember God's goodness toward us in the past, we put ourselves in the right posture for receiving joy from the sovereign Spirit. Joy is a gift we wait for.

But there's also an experiential explanation for why joy and hope can feel out of our grasp despite our best efforts. When we experience the loss, uncertainty, or fragility of the things we have loved, hoped in, or depended on for a sense of well-being, we often experience fear or shame. In these times, we're unsure of how to think about ourselves. When our identity and sense of self feel lost or fragile, we begin to wonder whether we can be enough. Curt Thompson, in his book *The Soul of Shame*, describes shame as "an undercurrent of sensed emotion, of which we may have either a slight or robust impression that, should we put words to it, would declare some version of *I am not enough; There is something wrong with me; I am bad;* or *I don't matter.*"[1]

Thompson, a clinical psychiatrist, explains that studies show how emotions like shame disintegrate the "temporal" capacity of the mind.[2] In other words, shame has a disabling power over our ability to reflect on our history and anticipate our future in a resourceful way. It steals our ability to give meaning to the history of our life and the potential of our future, narrowing us to a hopeless present. Shame disintegrates our ability to give witness to God's faithfulness. Gratitude and expectancy are stolen. Shame hamstrings us from practicing the basic strategies for finding joy that are laid out in Psalm 126. "Shame," explains Thompson, "wants very much to infect every element of the mind in order to distort God's story and offer another narrative."[3]

Shame can come at us in a myriad of ways, but as a pastor, I've noticed that there are two ordinary ones we ought to give some attention to—family and culture. Our family experience, especially during our childhood, deeply shapes how we experience the world. If these relationships are destructive or abusive, they can damage how we think about ourselves, the world, and God. For example, the way we experienced our fathers (or didn't experience them) shapes the way we perceive God as Father. And how we were received by our parents (mother or father) shapes how we believe we need to behave in order to be received by the world or by God.

My father was a fairly new believer when I was growing up. A very forceful memory I have is how he would regularly come beside my bed at night and ask for forgiveness for things he had said or done that day. Only as an adult have I realized how impactful that was for me. It wasn't his perfection that shaped me, but his willingness to admit (to his son, even) his imperfections and to repent. I can see now that this consistent behavior taught me it was normal to admit my failures and repent in the presence of God. I know that isn't everyone's experience. For some of us, our family history stirs shame, which works under the hood of our hearts, telling us, *This is how you should think about reality—about your past, your future.*

On top of this, our surrounding culture can deeply inform our view of the world and God. It can even disrupt what may have been an emotionally healthy family history. As I mentioned in chapter 4, self-hatred, or shame, is the true darkness of a performative society. In Matthew 23:1–12, Jesus condemns the scribes and the Pharisees. They were performative rather than genuine in their practices: "They do all their deeds to be seen by others" (v. 5). They loved to be greeted by others and honored at feasts and with exalted titles (vv. 6–7). But Jesus is angriest about the fact that their performance-oriented lives put inordinate burdens on others: "They tie up heavy burdens, hard to bear, and lay them on people's shoulders, but they themselves are not willing to move them with their finger" (v. 4).

A performative culture is crushing. Jonathan Haidt writes

about one example of this crushing weight of a performative world on teen girls:

> Social media—particularly Instagram, which displaces other forms of interaction among teens, puts the size of their friend group on public display, and subjects their physical appearance to the hard metrics of likes and comment counts—takes the worst parts of middle school and glossy women's magazines and intensifies them.[4]

One notable statistic Haidt shares is that "from 2010 to 2014, rates of hospital admission for self-harm did not increase at all for women in their early 20s, or for boys or young men, but they doubled for girls ages 10 to 14."[5]

The performative world can be emotionally and spiritually crushing. How can we find joy if our family history or surrounding culture crushes our spirits, promotes a sense of shame, and keeps us from recognizing God's good presence in the past and the future? Here are four strategies to discover joy in a fragile world.

1. Start with Self-Awareness

Curt Thompson points out that beginning to uproot the grip of shame "depends on how well we are paying attention to what we pay attention to."[6] I have found this truth to be vitally important. It's the most basic level of spiritual formation. Thompson observes, "Attention is the hallmark feature of this domain [of consciousness]."[7] For example, if our fathers shaped the way we experience God as Father, we should pay close attention to how we have experienced our fathers and how that informs the way we think about God.

I have watched lightbulbs go off in people's minds as they recognized this dynamic in their own lives. "I never connected those dots, but yes, I can see how my father's absence impacts my experience of God's presence." For some, it's the harshness of their father. For others, it's that their mother was impossible to please. Whatever the case may be, take time to recognize how much you are paying attention to the things your inner life focuses on, even subconsciously. For the most part, we haven't paid enough attention to this dynamic, despite the fact that it dictates the nature of so many of our relationships, including our relationship with God. We must pay attention to what we are paying attention to.

I remember about a decade ago being in Orlando after a large conference with other pastors and spiritual leaders. I was sitting at the hotel bar, catching up on emails and some work before heading to the airport. A friend who had about twenty years more experience than me in pastoral ministry sat down next to me. I was glad to see him. He had been at the same church for a long time and seemingly had a fruitful and happy life, so I asked what had been helpful along the way. He seemed to know immediately. About ten years into his work, he almost quit. He felt everyone was critical of his work, and he felt like he couldn't please anyone. He came to his elders ready to resign since he concluded he just wasn't a good fit. This news confused his elders, who admired and loved their pastor. Instead of receiving his resignation, they encouraged him to seek counseling.

This friend had actually been receiving healthy feedback about his weaknesses, but he was receiving it through the filter of the experience of his broken family life growing up and his inability to be close to his parents. When he heard criticism, his heart was paying attention to his lack of acceptance from his father and mother. Recognizing that dynamic was a game changer for him.

But it's important to understand that this self-awareness is not the same thing as transformation. Once we've noticed how our family history has informed our responses to God, we must then allow God to define who he is *apart from* our experience with our families. Or once we've noticed what our culture tells us to be afraid of, sorry for, or ashamed of, we must allow God to speak his truth to us.

Here we see the importance of our initial emphasis in chapter 1 concerning a secret life with the Father (see Matthew 6). Only there, in that secret place of thunder, can we disrupt our familial and culturally informed shame. There we experience his presence. So let me emphasize this point: Self-awareness is not sufficient for transformation; we need God's presence for healing.

2. Abide in God's Presence

God's presence is an important part of experiencing God's healing joy. In the Old Testament, a central theme is *God's presence with God's people.* "More even than the law, therefore, or other identity markers such as circumcision, food laws, and Sabbath observance," writes Bible scholar Gordon Fee, "God's presence with Israel distinguished them as his people."[8]

The big tragedy of Exodus 32 is the Israelites' impatience while Moses is on Mount Sinai and their turning away from God to worship the golden calf. God responds in anger, saying he'll send an angel with them on their journey to the promised land but he won't go with them himself. And so Moses responds, saying essentially, "If you won't go with us, we aren't leaving." He amplifies further: "For how shall it be known that I have found favor in your sight, I and your people? Is it not in your going with us, so that we are distinct, I and your people, from every other people on the face of the earth?" (Exodus 33:16).

Moses knew *God's presence* would distinguish them as a people, not their law, their cultural distinctions, or their food or dress codes. Their moral obedience and social identity markers wouldn't set them apart as God's people. Those things could all be performed and appropriated. Moses and the Israelites needed something deeper for transformation and renewal.

The outward appearance of having things together is void of power. The promise of our performative culture today is that if people work to organize their life to look just right, the rest will follow.[9] Our culture trains us to believe the performance of the self is more important than the reality.

As I write this chapter, I am currently in Louisville, Kentucky, preaching for a friend who is on sabbatical. In the first half of the service as we were singing, down the middle aisle came a woman, laboring to walk to the front. She sat down on the front row. She was obviously struggling, physically and possibly emotionally. I thought at first she was looking for someone to talk to, but no, she was simply finding her seat. She sat as we were all standing and singing. She mouthed the words and looked as if she couldn't sit comfortably. But soon

I could tell that everyone around her recognized her. Many waved, and she slowly stood so she could move closer to hug some of them.

Afterward, I asked about her, and while the details aren't mine to share, I heard a story of a woman who had undergone many painful trials. In the eyes of the world, she was not very impressive as she made her way into church. But I couldn't help but notice how so many people around her deeply loved and admired her, not in spite of her weakness, but for how she embodied it. She wasn't *doing* remarkable things. But she was able to receive her life in the presence of Christ. She became a beautiful witness to the goodness of God.

This is why Jesus emphasized in Matthew 6 the dangers of having an outward appearance of godliness without a secret life with the Father. Outward appearances of mercy, public prayer, and fasting are important parts of being a Christian, but the substance of the Christian life is God's presence.[10] There we will find healing for shame, and with that healing, fresh hope—and with hope, joy.

3. Receive Joy in the Wilderness

As Psalm 126 continues, it shifts toward expressing the psalmist's prayers and longings to God. Psalm 126:4 says, "Restore our fortunes, O LORD, like streams in the Negeb!" This prayer is both realistic and hopeful.

It's realistic because it comes from the psalmist as he reckons with his circumstances. The Negeb is a desert region in southern Israel. The psalmist recognizes that his circumstances are like a wilderness, and trying to get joy and hope out of his circumstances is like trying to find streams of water among the wilderness rocks. But the psalmist is holding a spiritual tension that will sustain him in his trouble—he is cynical about his life but not about God. His circumstances are a wasteland, but God is with him. So he prays, "Restore our fortunes, O LORD, like streams in the Negeb!"

The psalmist is not simply asking for his old comforts back or that his circumstances would revert to happier times. Deeper than that, he's asking for joy *out of his wilderness moment.* He's not asking for a change of circumstance; he's asking for the ability to receive joy, hope, and abundance from something other than his circumstance. He's asking for divine intervention in the midst of emptiness. He's looking for the joy of spiritual vitality in a valley of death.

An inner transformation has happened in the gap between the psalmist not being able to imagine a hopeful future to now imagining a miraculous one. He remembers God's faithful history, his shame is healed by God's presence, and he asks for restoration in the hope that God might do a mighty work again. Artur Weiser points out that within this pathway of transformation "lies the strength of faith which alone gives the community the spiritual authority to utter such a petition and so makes this prayer profoundly devout and humble."[11]

Old comforts and success are too fragile to sustain the psalmist's joy and hope. He needs something deeper and more vibrant. He doesn't simply need to get his life together and give an outward appearance of success to impress the nations again. He longs for a supernatural encounter with God. He wants revival.

4. Sow Your Tears

The psalmist ends with one more counterintuitive strategy
for joy:

> Those who sow in tears
> shall reap with shouts of joy!
> He who goes out weeping,
> bearing the seed for sowing,
> shall come home with shouts of joy,
> bringing his sheaves with him.
> (Psalm 126:5–6)

The psalmist instructs us to sow our tears. We give our tears
to the Lord, and the Lord plants them like seeds. God actually
transforms our tears, our losses, our groans, and our griefs into
joy. I don't know how he does it. But what we are asked to do
is simple and straightforward—practice the ordinary rhythm of
lament.

Lament is a Christian practice of giving our griefs and sorrows to God. The psalms are filled with laments. They give
grieving Christians words to say when they can't find any.[12] God
has inspired words in the Bible to speak to him when our lives
are falling apart. He encourages us to sing our questions, our
confusions, and even our accusations to him in order that he
might use our sorrows like seeds and bury them in the soil of his
love for us.

I find it immeasurably comforting that God wants us to
hand over our griefs to him. God is not the author of our evils,

but he is the redeemer of our trials. He takes seriously even the losses in our performative world. It's not that God thinks our money or freedoms are all that serious. What he does take seriously is our broken hearts.

This is resurrection work, of course. Just as the Father buried his Son like a seed in the ground, so he sows our tears. And just as his Son's death bears unimaginable fruit, so he turns our sorrows into resurrection joys. Again, I don't know how he does this, but just as he turned the terrible cross of his Son, Jesus Christ, into the hope of the world, he takes our tears that feel like death and turns them into a harvest of joy. If he can raise his Son to life, he can turn our weeping into laughing.

But we don't get a harvest of joy without the sowing of tears. If we merely try to "keep it light," escaping or numbing our pain, or just gritting our teeth and bearing it, we will miss the harvest. Our tears are seeds. For a long time, Christians have known what to do with their grief and pain—we lament. We open the book of Psalms to the laments and pray, slowing down to align our thoughts, experiences, and emotions with a history of Christian sufferers who have formed and learned the language of sowing tears.[13]

Lament is difficult because it allows raw emotions to surface. Our impulse is to reach for our phone or some other measure of escape to numb the things we don't want to feel. But allowing difficult emotions to surface in the presence of God and God's people is how we experience healing. Eugene Peterson writes:

> One of the most interesting and remarkable things Christians
> learn is that laughter does not exclude weeping. Christian joy

is not an escape from sorrow. Pain and hardship still come, but they are unable to drive out the happiness of the redeemed.

A common but futile strategy for achieving joy is trying to eliminate things that hurt: get rid of pain by numbing the nerve ends, get rid of insecurity by eliminating risks, get rid of disappointment by depersonalizing your relationships. And then try to lighten the boredom of such a life by buying joy in the form of vacations and entertainment. There isn't a hint of that in Psalm 126.[14]

God won't simply replace our tears with joy. Our tears, themselves, become a path to joy.

Chapter 6

ABIDING OVER OPTIMIZING

We are in the era of what Alexandra Schwartz calls "the hard doctrine of personal optimization."[1] Gone are the days of the power of positive thinking, from Norman Vincent Peale to Rhonda Byrne's *The Secret*, where you were encouraged to, as Schwartz explains, "clean out a closet for the man of your dreams and imagine him hanging up his ties" if you wanted a husband, or "picture yourself acing your next vision exam" if you wanted to get rid of your glasses.[2] Whether it was God or the universe you were sending your wish out to, the assumption was that the world was generally bent toward optimism and success, and all you had to do was align yourself with it to participate in the abundance. Resist negative thoughts, and trouble will flee from you.

But today we live in a different era. We are not as optimistic about the world's generosity. As mentioned in chapter 1, a whole generation of young adults have come to adulthood between the bookends of a 2008 recession and a 2020 pandemic, with political, social, and racial turmoil; unsteady job markets; and burdensome school debt sandwiched between. For many, the world seems indifferent to our good vibes. But that hasn't kept us from trying to get what we want or to become who we think we should become. The new gurus we seek out to help us maximize our potential are psychologists, tech entrepreneurs, and sociologists who come not with messages of optimism but with data and metrics. "It's no longer enough," says Schwartz, "to imagine our way to a better state of body or mind. We must now chart our progress, count our steps, log our sleep rhythms, tweak our diets, record our negative thoughts—then analyze the data, recalibrate, and repeat."[3]

We have books that tell us how to make good habits and then get the most productivity out of them (see *The Power of Habit* by Charles Duhigg), or how to stay motivated when times are tough (see Duhigg's follow-up, *Smarter Faster Better*; Angela Duckworth's *Grit*; or Jane McGonigal's *SuperBetter*). We have books that help us aim toward getting done what's most important to us (see *Essentialism* by Greg McKeown) and then how to make the most important things easier (see McKeown's follow-up, *Effortless*). There are books on how to prioritize our mental energy for maximal productivity (see Cal Newport's *Deep Work*) and how to resist digital distractions that threaten it (see Newport's follow-up, *Digital Minimalism*). There is no end to optimizing wisdom in areas ranging from our sex lives to our spirituality, from our creative energy to our money management, from our parenting to our friendships. Travel, wealth, food, organization, exercise, and more are all areas in our lives waiting to be optimized, along with a life coach just a DM away.

The formula looks something like this: We desire a certain kind of life, but we experience limitations or setbacks that prevent us from attaining it. We then seek ways to optimize ourselves to overcome our limitations and actualize the life we want. We not only want to experience this life but also want to demonstrate it before others in order to help shape a public identity and sense of self-worth. This likely isn't a conscious life plan for many of us, but it's one we've very likely digested and implemented along the way.

As we've already noted, our society gives us all kinds of conflicting messages—be more productive *and* have a more balanced life; be more fit *and* post pictures of yourself at all the restaurants; be a good parent *and* don't let anyone get in the way of your ambitions. We can never live up to these ideals, but at least we have Instagram, where we can post pictures to give people the impression that we are making it. As British journalist Will Storr points out in his book *Selfie*, the pressure to live up to a standard of perfection that our culture is pushing us toward is actually killing us.[4] We are comparing ourselves to an ideal self that isn't realistic or healthy, and we end up optimizing things we shouldn't. For many of us, optimization has led to diminishment.

To be clear, I have read and benefited from most of the books mentioned above. I want to be productive and find meaningful strategies to help me resist wasting time on things that take me away from the important things in life. I want to finish my week feeling as if I've accomplished something and participated in meaningful activities. There is wisdom to be found in these books, to be sure. But our performative society can diminish that wisdom into a destructive vision of a life that weighs us down and crushes us. It turns longings for a life of meaning and significance into vanity and hollowness.

Our world doesn't distinguish well between a productive life and a meaningful one, between efficiency and significance. The New Testament's vision of life is unique in that it resists the language of productivity and efficiency, not because it is wrong or evil, but because it's inadequate to contain the significance and substance our desires are reaching for. Instead, Jesus uses the language of "bearing fruit." Here we find imagery sufficient to make sense of our desires.

The Inefficient Process
of Growing Fruit

The longest explanation of what this life looks like is found in John 15. Jesus describes it within the context of chapters 13–17, where Jesus is eating a last meal with his disciples while preparing them for what is ahead—his crucifixion. The world is about to collapse around them, and Jesus has a few concentrated hours left to prepare them for what's about to happen. They will be called to build the church and commanded to reach the ends of the earth with the message of the Messiah.

Yet Jesus does not offer a grand strategic plan for how to plant churches, how to evangelize, how to defend the truth of the resurrection, how to structure future church governance, or even how to escape the weight of Roman persecution. It's not a how-to talk, despite the fact that they will have much to do and they are all still pretty clueless. In fact, for how much the disciples were called to do, there wasn't any discussion of productivity. Instead, Jesus takes up most of the time washing their feet and talking about the Trinity.[5] And he talks about bearing fruit. You can't help but wonder at how *inefficient* all of this is.

He tells his disciples, "I am the vine; you are the branches. Whoever abides in me and I in him, he it is that bears much fruit, for apart from me you can do nothing" (John 15:5). The imagery of fruitfulness carries with it a *thick* sense of living rather than a *thin* sense. Jesus is leading us to something deeper than the project of self—toward participation with him. Plant your life *in me*, he tells us.

I am suggesting that, over the loud clamor of our society, before we optimize anything, we should consider what kind of life

Jesus wants for us. We have already mentioned that he has a vision of a life, much of it in secret with the Father, that isn't built on what we think the world will be impressed with. But he also wants us to be *fruitful*. But while our culture may imagine a fruitful life to be equivalent to a productive life, Jesus has something different in mind. Here are a few things he points out about fruitful living.

A Life of Deep Love

John 15:10 explains that abiding with Christ means abiding in his love. This life of love that Jesus calls us into is meant to look like his life of love with the Father. It comes from abiding in him. The language of *abiding* evokes long-term, unhurried togetherness. That's where love is born and intimacy thrives. Our performative world teaches us optimization as a way of life in order to achieve what we were "made for." But Jesus teaches us that we were made for a life of love with him, and our abiding must never be optimized.

Abiding is slow and unproductive. I don't know how to get around this. There's no shortage of advice about how to fit spiritual exercises and disciplines into a busy life. You can listen to Scripture while you wash dishes or go for a run. You can read through a prayer book on the train. A friend of mine would bring a book of prayers with him every time he had to excuse himself to use the restroom. There's nothing wrong with these efforts to fit more Scripture and moments of prayer into our lives. But a life of love is generally not formed through multitasking. If I want to have a life of deep love and intimacy with my spouse, it comes through long, unhurried times together. Those times won't seem like they're very productive or even efficient. The same is true of our relationship with God.

Expectant Prayer

John 15:7 reads, "If you abide in me, and my words abide in you, ask whatever you wish, and it will be done for you." I have increasingly found the practice of expectant prayer to be important in my life with God. Our abiding with Christ will give way to love, our love will give way to desires, and our desires will give way to asking. We are called to a life of love and welcome: "Ask whatever you want."

I want to talk more deeply about what this command to ask with expectancy might look like, but first we must grasp that this life of prayer comes from a life of love. The fruit of abiding and loving is a sense that God welcomes our longings and desires. To put it differently, Jesus wants us to embrace a vision of the good life in which we experience deep, abiding love and the satisfaction of our desires.

A Life in Which God Gets the Glory

John 15:8 reveals that the fruit of a life of love and the satisfaction of our desires is that God gets glory from our lives. Jesus talks this way in Matthew 5, where people see evidence of this love and expectancy in your life and they praise, not you, but God (see Matthew 5:15–16). This means that a life of love and the satisfaction of desires is not a performative life; it is a life that produces *worship*. We become people who don't anxiously grasp for what they *want* in this world but who experience joy in what God *gives*. Your life stops witnessing to *your* success and the spoils that everyone envies and starts witnessing to the *goodness of God* that everyone is invited to receive.

The fruit of being with Christ is that your life becomes attractive—not the kind of life that is posted or published and everyone comments, "I want your life!" but a life that compels other people, as they experience your presence in ordinary settings, to long for what you have. You become a means through which others can experience the power and presence of Christ.

If you've read this far into the book, I imagine this kind of life is deeply attractive to you. But many of us are experiencing the frenzied anxiety of a performative life rather than the joy and peace resulting from a life of love and fruitfulness. Jesus is describing a spiritually enlarged existence, but often we are more familiar with the distractions and diminishments of a world that pushes us toward continual efforts to secure a stable identity. Those who give themselves over to this Babylonian, performative world end up finding that their lives have insufficient content or meaning to it. It's frail and hollow.

Vitality in Christ

It's significant that Jesus' command in John 15 is not to bear fruit but to *abide*, to be with Christ in the same way a branch is with a vine. The main ingredient to this life that Christ imagines for us is abiding. Jesus again uses the agrarian imagery of fruitfulness to help us see—seeds and soil, branches and vines. The *result* of abiding is fruitfulness. But the *substance* behind it all dwells in unseen places where seeds are hidden in dirt and a branch is connected to a vine. It is the hidden nature of our life with God that animates us, not the demonstration of our achievements. Even deeper than that, Jesus is pointing out that the substance of our spiritual life is that we are *with him* rather than what we are *doing for him*.

The vitality of the soil to a seed or a vine to a branch isn't noticeable or dramatic. But we all know a branch cannot be fruitful while it's lying on the ground. The branch cannot be what it was made to be unless it abides in the vine. Jesus is trying to help us understand our relationship with him. His relationship with us is like a head with a body. A life system runs from the head to the ends of the hands and feet. Jesus has an infinite amount of spiritual vitality in him—a bottomless well of healing and wholeness. To break away from him is death.

But even while many of us do not break away from Christ, we often look for our vitality in other sources. Our experience of his joy and the fullness of his life gets clogged up by our abiding in other things. It's no wonder that optimizing our lives in order to achieve and to demonstrate those achievements is so wearying. There's *no life* in it. It depletes us, sapping us of spiritual vibrancy.

The previous chapter revealed that we need to "pay attention to what we pay attention to." We also need to pay attention to the things that are clogging up our abiding with Christ. Are you paying attention to Christ in a *vital* way? Let me give you an example of what I mean.

Consider the story of Jesus as he stood before his accusers in Matthew 27. Prior to this story, in chapter 26, Jesus was arrested and brought before Caiaphas the high priest, where many tried to bear false witness against him in order to put him to death. The predominant theme of that episode is that against all the false testimony, "Jesus remained silent" (Matthew 26:63). In Matthew 27, when Jesus is finally brought before Pilate, this theme of his silence continues: "But when he was accused by the chief priests and elders, he gave no answer" (v. 12). Pilate presses him, "'Do you not hear how many things they testify against you?' But he gave him no answer, not even to a single charge, so that the governor was greatly amazed" (vv. 13–14). Matthew wants us to notice: "Jesus remained silent" (26:63); "he gave no answer" (27:12); "he gave him no answer," reemphasizing, "not even to a single charge" (v. 14).

Why was Jesus silent? If we were witnesses to these events, what might we think? Maybe he became resigned to the fact that nothing he could say would change the minds of his accusers or Pilate. Jesus had watched John the Baptist be unjustly murdered, and perhaps he assumed it was fruitless to resist what was coming.

Or maybe it was indifference. He had spent his entire ministry communicating truth, healing the sick, and caring for the poor, yet he had been constantly slandered, attacked, and questioned by the religious leaders. Maybe he was done. He just didn't care anymore.

But resignation and indifference weren't the story here, as the prophecy in Isaiah 53 shows us:

> He was oppressed, and he was afflicted,
>   yet he opened not his mouth;
> like a lamb that is led to the slaughter,
>   and like a sheep that before its shearers
>   is silent,
>   so he opened not his mouth. (Isaiah 53:7)

Matthew sees in Jesus the fulfillment of the Suffering Servant described by the prophet Isaiah. Jesus was involved in something deeper than just a story of mishandled justice; he was fulfilling his calling as the Suffering Servant. He was being

121

obedient to the Father. He was living out the purpose for his coming. Jesus wasn't getting caught up in the schemes of the scribes and the Pharisees to destroy him. His enemies were being unwittingly included in the eternal plan of the Suffering Lamb. Jesus wasn't silent out of indifference or resignation. Isaiah 50:7 describes this Suffering Servant as one whose face was set "like a flint" in unwavering determination to persevere in obedience to what was before him.

Have you ever been struck by someone whose sense of calling was so deep that they persevered in profound ways? I've recently been reading about Cecil B. Moore, a defense attorney who worked for a decade for Black Philadelphians to have equal access to education, housing, and jobs—to have the same rights and receive the same respect as their White neighbors. There is a winsome beauty in lives like that. How much more beautiful is Christ in his perseverance? "He was oppressed, and he was afflicted, yet he opened not his mouth" (Isaiah 53:7). His silence speaks of his resiliency.

In addition to obedience, Jesus was driven by trust. He trusted the Father to vindicate him, refusing to place his hope in his words before the council or Pilate. Jesus "did not entrust himself" to other humans (John 2:24). He trusted in something deeper than human approval and praise. He trusted that in the end, he would be declared to be in the right, regardless of human opinion or whether courts of law sided with him in that moment. Jesus knew that the evil schemes, power, and slander of the religious leaders and the condemnation of Pilate would not have the last word. In this moment of great emotional intensity, Jesus remained silent and did not act on any perceived need to vindicate himself.

I find it striking how profoundly Jesus was governed by his trust in the Father over against what people thought of him. It's hard for many of us to even walk into a room without feeling the sharp impulse to vindicate ourselves. Even if we don't hear a single slight or word of slander from others, we often imagine what others are thinking about us. We compensate for how others may interpret our weaknesses. We talk more than we need to in order to display a degree of intelligence. We overwork in order to show others how truly needed and indispensable we are. We don't need literal condemnations or false accusations from others to fall into this state; we do a good job inventing those things on our own.

We entrust ourselves so deeply to the approval and praise of others that the silence of Jesus in this trial story seems otherworldly. But Jesus lived solely on the love and vindication of his Father. When the approval and praise of the world were gone, he didn't fall apart. He didn't even open his mouth. What a beautiful life. His silence speaks of his trust.

But beyond his resiliency and trust, he was driven by love, of course. How beautiful this love is! Look at how Isaiah 53 unpacks his love: "He has borne our griefs and carried our sorrows (v. 4); "he was pierced for our transgressions; he was crushed for our iniquities," which "brought us peace" (v. 5); he heals us with his wounds (v. 5); he laid our iniquities on himself (v. 6); and he prays for our forgiveness (v. 12). The beauty of Jesus' silence before Pilate was that he was governed more by love than by anxiety. The future didn't make Jesus anxious because he was led by his love.

When I was young, anxiety was a helpful motivator toward accomplishment. You can get a lot done and achieve much based on fear. It can take you to the ends of the earth sometimes. But as I've gotten older, I've noticed that my anxiety, while a great motivator for productivity, is a hindrance to love.

Our anxieties come from various sources—the culture we've embodied, the stories we've inherited, the wounds we've received, the ambitions that consume us, and the comforts we crave. Often people, especially those closest to us, experience the pain of our anxieties. The people in our lives become barriers to our peace and obstacles to the things we want to make happen. Sometimes anxiety becomes a governing dynamic in our lives, making love extremely difficult to express or even feel. I'm sure many of you can relate.

That's why the silence of Jesus is so beautiful to me. He is ruled by love more than anxiety. He doesn't have ambitions that keep him from loving me. I am not an obstacle to what he really wants or a barrier to his hopes. Oh, how he loves us. His silence is beautiful because it speaks of his love.

Isn't his silence amazing? Even Pilate was amazed, but his amazement produced no lasting or transformative fruit in him. Something deeper than the amazement of Pilate is being asked of us. What does it mean to give vital attention to the beauty of Jesus' silence so that something deeper than superficial amazement occurs?

Abiding in the silence of Jesus means holding it with us and allowing his resilience to speak to our frailty, his trust to touch our insecurities, and his love to comfort our anxieties. Paying vital attention to the silence of Jesus enables it to challenge our speech and transform us. We are moved to new longings—*Oh, that I was more like the silence of Jesus!*—asking the Spirit to awaken us to all that we are and all that we possess in Christ.

An ordinary way to pay vital attention to and abide with Christ is to meditate on his beauty, allowing it to confront our sins, heal our wounds, and transform us from one degree of glory to the next. And in this abiding, we bear much fruit. But apart from it, we can produce nothing but a fruitless amazement like that of Pilate.

What Do You Want?

In this context of abiding, Jesus instructs us to "ask whatever you wish" (John 15:7). These words can be startling to read, especially since this open invitation is followed by the assurance, "and it will be done for you." What grabs our attention is the "ask whatever you wish," and it bewilders us. But the first part is the key: "If you abide in me, and my words abide in you . . ." Jesus is trying to get us to imagine a relationship with him so deep that our automatic impulse is to bring him our desires, to stop qualifying our words or approaching him with an overly cautious posture, to define our asking by our abiding.

That relationship means, though, that we must be *with* Christ for more than just the times when we come to *ask for whatever we want*. In other words, our abiding becomes more characteristic of us than our asking, and our asking becomes more informed and characterized by our abiding. This is a communion-driven relationship, not a transactional one. The abiding begins to transform our wants. The people I know with the most intimate relationship with Christ have the fewest qualifications in their requests to God. They simply ask with unreserved *expectancy*. This passage is not about, *How do I get what I want?* Rather, it's about, *How do I get Christ? And when I get Christ, how can I find the confidence and freedom to ask what I want?*

To be honest, I don't quite know what to make of the seemingly open-ended invitation to ask for whatever we desire and Jesus' unqualified confidence that we'll receive it. Explanations for why we don't seem to experience this kind of ask-receive dynamic often either minimize the generosity Jesus communicates or put too much weight on our spiritual qualifications to make something happen from God. Either God isn't as generous as he says he is, or we aren't as faithful as we need to be. These explanations miss the tone and direction of the heart of Jesus.

It's interesting that Jesus ended his time with his disciples emphasizing their wants and desires, since that is what he began with. At the beginning of John's gospel, as two of John the Baptist's disciples began to follow Jesus, he turned and asked a pointed question: "What are you seeking?" (John 1:38). Jesus also asks us this fundamental question: *What do you want?* When we follow Jesus, he is interested not simply in our belief systems or the substance of what we know. He doesn't ask his first disciples, "What do you believe?" James K. A. Smith explains, "Discipleship, we might say, is a way to curate your heart, to be attentive to and intentional about what you love. So discipleship is more a matter of hungering and thirsting than of knowing and believing."[6]

If this emphasis on desire functions as bookends to the disciples' time with Jesus in his ministry, I wonder if it can help us understand what happened in between. Jesus performed miracles with bread (John 6:1–15) and wine (John 2:1–12), talked to an alienated woman with a sexually complicated past about her thirsts (John 4:1–30), and called himself "the bread of life" who satisfies all who hunger (John 6:22–35). Throughout his ministry and teaching, he confronted people's longings and desires, expectations and hopes. Remember his postresurrection breakfast meal with Peter after he disowned Jesus three times? Jesus asked Peter *three times*, "Do you love me?" (Again, note that Jesus didn't ask, "Now will you obey me?" or "Now will you be faithful?")

Here's what I am suggesting: Life with Jesus confronts my desires—*what are you seeking?*—and satisfies my desires—*ask whatever you wish*. Both are part of our abiding with Jesus. We are not asked to simply die to our wants, and we are not promised merely the satisfaction of our wants. Jesus has a deep interest in our desires, both the shaping and the fulfillment of them. In him, our desires are purified and satisfied.

This fundamental question—*what do you want?*—is the difference between a productive and a fruitful life. Productivity doesn't ask the confronting question about our desires; it just aims to provide the most effective way to get them. But Jesus directs our attention to a deeper life of fruitfulness that demands a *transformation* of our desires. He points our imagination to a life that experiences not only the satisfaction of our desires (John 15:7) but also the pain of *pruning*: "Every branch that does bear fruit he prunes, that it may bear more fruit" (v. 2).

The Father's Pruning

Somehow Jesus imagines that within the same life with him, we experience the pain of pruning along with the joy of asking. It's a counterintuitive image. The Father is like the vinedresser of our lives, who knows that a grapevine full of foliage might be beautiful, but it won't be fruitful. It won't fulfill the purpose of its existence—namely, fruitfulness. An experienced and wise vinedresser prunes the foliage back. It's an essential part of renewing the vine.

A pruned vine is not very pretty. What previously looked vibrant and beautiful is cut down to stubs. If you listen to a vinedresser (or viticulturalist, as we call them in the US) talk about pruning, they describe it as *wounding*. Cutting the vine down is "opening a wound," making the plant susceptible to diseases, especially during wet seasons. Pruning a vine strips it of its beauty and makes it more vulnerable, but it also ensures that it will be more fruitful in the future.

Jesus assumes we will experience something like this in our lives with him. For spiritual vitality and fruitfulness, we often need a stripping away of what *feels* beautiful in our lives, what *seems* needed. This is difficult. A pruned life in Christ feels like death. It strips away the things we're connected to. We experience the pain of losing things we've depended on for life, productivity, and happiness. But while these things seem important, beautiful, and necessary, in reality they're keeping us away from true joy and fruitfulness. Pruning feels like death, but it leads to life and fruitfulness.

Here, then, is one of the severe dangers of a performative life: It cannot abide pruning. If we simply follow along with the performative individualism of our world, the necessary and seasonal pruning of the Father will be intolerable. How could it not be? Remember the conversation Jesus had with the rich young man in Matthew 19? If our sense of self-worth is based in our ability to demonstrate our impressive lives before others, we will resist Christ and resent the Father's pruning hands.

But if we want to experience fruitfulness, even into old age, and if we want the Father's will for our lives rather than simply the outcome of our own plans and ambitions, then our lives will sometimes need some pruning. We will experience weakness. People will not always think we are impressive. We will experience the loss of things we consider vital to our future. We might lose our reputation or status. We might lose our health. Close friends may slander us. Our enemies might win. We might experience a deep and sudden grief that throws us into immediate confusion and panic, or we might experience a long season of slow and steady losses that morph into a deep soul fatigue.

But when these seasons come—and they will—they come not from an indifferent and careless Father who dismisses our pain. We may think God has abandoned us, or we may assume he is not good. We may grow bitter and hardened for a while, but God is at work, cutting back what is standing in the way of a long life of growth and fruit.

We can trust Jesus' words here because as he said them, he was preparing himself for the cross. He trusted the Father's hands. He knew what was on the other side, and it was his joy. That's why on the cross, the moment of ultimate pain and pruning, he had the wherewithal to say to the Father, "Into your hands I commit my spirit!" (Luke 23:46). Older, more mature Christians often see in past seasons of great pain and loss evidences of where God was at work. Much of the fruit comes from paying attention to and trusting the hands of the Father. They are good hands.

For those of us who live in a performative age, Jesus is warning us, *Don't believe the promises of this Babylonian world. Don't follow the patterns and ambitions that you have embraced or digested along the way.* To be fruitful, we must experience pruning, and it is never on our terms.

In our performative age, we can demonstrate a kind of vulnerability—a social media influencer can post a video with no makeup and talk about mental health and body image. We can display our weakness and still be praised, be called brave. Some of us are very good at this. If you've been a Christian long enough, you likely know the right words and posture to carry out the act of a righteous sufferer. But this apparent weakness we exhibit before others is on our terms. We are in control of what is seen and what isn't, what is known and not known. But a branch cannot prune itself, and neither can we.

Jesus is trying to prepare us intellectually, emotionally, and spiritually for a kind of pruning that is not on our terms. We may not want it at all. But if it is received by faith, it will be for our good. Jesus wants us to remember his words to his disciples in John 15:11: "These things I have spoken to you, that my joy may be in you, and that your joy may be full." We can miss a few obvious things in what Jesus is telling us if we're not careful. In the Bible, especially the Old Testament, a grapevine was one of God's means for his people's joy. The prophets use this imagery when trying to explain the good life: "Everyone will sit under their own vine and under their own fig tree, and no one will make them afraid" (Micah 4:4 NIV; see also 1 Kings 4:25; Zechariah 3:10). As Psalm 104:14–15 tells us, God provides bread for strength and wine for joy! A deep part of experiencing God's blessedness is experiencing the fruit of the vine.

And what does Jesus say? "I am the vine" (John 15:5). *I am for your joy. Don't go to other vines.* He wants us to experience *his joy*—that "my joy may be in you" (v. 11). All the infinite love and happiness he experiences with the Father, he wants you to have. The Father's goal for your life is for you to be as joyful as the glorified Christ in heaven. Receive, then, the pruning as God's gentle hand. Let him take away what's dead to make room for life. You will never regret it.

Chapter 7

STAGNANT GRACE

Two weeks into my new life as a pastor, a Sunday worship service had ended and one of the church members asked to speak to me urgently. We sat down, away from everybody, and he said, "Pastor, I plan on leaving my wife soon, and I need your help to keep the drama down and the hurt to a minimum." I sat there and blinked. I asked if he could hold off with his plans until we could talk more. He agreed. We met again the following day, and he told me his story.

This man had a radical conversion story from a painful family history, drug abuse, alcoholism, and depression to a profound encounter with God. He told of miracles and stories of grace. He then told me how he met his wife and how God provided amazing opportunities and favor at his job. His story was of one victory and miracle after another. There was so much joy in his voice as he recounted what God had done—I couldn't believe his words were leading up to how he wanted to create a shipwreck of it all.

When he finally began to tell me why he planned to leave his wife, he explained that he hadn't felt God's presence in years. God seemed to have stopped working. His marriage had grown cold, and many resentments had built up between the two of them. He'd undergone many failures and embarrassments at work, including a demotion. He needed a fresh start. He said he needed to find a new church, with a new community, in order to hear God's voice again and experience a fresh sense of God's power.

Thankfully, the man never followed through on his plan to abandon his family and his church community. But it took some years for him to settle into the season in which God had placed him. What I've grown to appreciate about this story is that while it's true that if he had followed through with this plans, he would have caused a lot of pain, it's also true that he was simply saying out loud what many of us feel in the quiet parts of our hearts in certain times and seasons of our lives.

This story hints at an important principle for spiritual maturity. *A life where Christ has the significant upper hand in the formation of your identity demands that there be what I call stagnant seasons.* You need periods of both vulnerability and stillness. The difficult thing about stagnant seasons in a performative culture is that they produce nothing impressive to display. Our impulse during these seasons is to *make something happen*, but spiritual maturity demands that we resist this impulse and receive each season as a grace.

One of these moments happens in John 21. It's an intimate story—Peter and Jesus talking over a charcoal fire. We see something profound happen here. It's a deeply sensitive story. Things get brought up in this conversation that raise painful emotions. But Jesus never brings up anything he doesn't intend to heal.

The Slow Times

The story begins with the phrase "After this" (John 21:1). In other words, this is *post* something significant. It occurs after the cross and resurrection of Jesus, which was a monumental moment, of course, but it also happened after the Feast of Unleavened Bread.

All of Israel was in Jerusalem. It was a heightened religious scene, with everyone present for a weeklong feast—a cultural moment of concentrated political and religious energy. Think New Year's Eve in Times Square, but all week long. Add to that a controversial figure coming into a crowded Jerusalem riding on a donkey and people responding with intense emotion, wanting to crown him king. As the Pharisees watched these things play out, they said to themselves, "Look, the world has gone after him" (John 12:19).

By the end of the feast week, Jesus had been abruptly arrested and sentenced to public execution, this turn of events bringing with it a whiplash of emotion. At the cross, there is a mix of triumphant mockery and severe grief. Jesus died and was buried. And then, at the beginning of the following week, he rose from the dead, revealing himself to his closest friends and disciples. Suddenly a new hope was birthed, and a new world was anticipated! This was a week of intense significance, grief, and excitement.

John 21 takes place "after this." The feast was over, emotions had come down, and everyone was going home. Things weren't moving at breakneck speed anymore. Praise God that Jesus is alive! But what now?

The world around the followers of Jesus hadn't changed much. Jerusalem had been full of people with religious and emotional fervor, but Jesus hadn't revealed himself to them. Now they were going home.

At this point, the disciples' minds may have been starting to focus on their embarrassing failures in the heat of important moments with Jesus. They had abandoned him during his arrest. When it mattered most, they scattered, escaped, denied involvement, and washed their hands of the matter. Like Pilate, they didn't want to be involved in or responsible for what happened to Jesus. So at Jesus' return, his followers experienced excitement and hope, but in the back of their minds was the nagging suggestion that they didn't deserve to participate in what was going to happen going forward.

So "after this," they went back to fishing. They put their heads down and went back to their old job. You can understand that desire after a particularly embarrassing failure: *Just do something I'm good at. Get an easy win.* So they got into a boat and paddled out to the middle of the Sea of Tiberias.

Except they couldn't even get a win there. They didn't catch a thing. Maybe being on the road with Jesus those three years had caused their fishing skills to atrophy. Or maybe they were simply disillusioned about themselves. That kind of emotional weight can make even the simplest of tasks hard. Either way, they were moving from failure to failure. That's when Jesus entered the scene.

Here is an important spiritual insight to consider: Emotionally heightened seasons are good. A lot can happen when everyone is together, when things are happening and God is working. Maybe you remember seasons of great power and spiritual energy in your younger years. Perhaps you remember times in college when you would stay up late with friends, studying the Bible and praying. Everything seemed heightened with God's presence. Prayers were answered, and your faith seemed to climb. You spoke boldly about your relationship with Christ. You felt as if anything could happen—and sometimes it did!

Or maybe you experienced seasons at church when God was building something significant. Fruit seemed to be low-hanging, and everyone had a part to play. Lives were changed. You witnessed miracles. Times of worship were filled with power, and every moment felt like a burning bush.

But now things feel very different. Life has returned to a normal pace and you're living a more ordinary life, wondering if God is still at work. When people move to New York City, they're often following a dream. They imagine the perfect job—sitting in an office or studio with a cityscape view, going to shows, eating at glamorous restaurants with attractive people. But when they arrive, reality often sets in. Maybe their office is dark, and their window faces a brick wall of another building. They take the same crowded subway commute every morning and evening and order the same takeout every night. Their lives are at the mercy of the mundane.

Things aren't quite *moving* the way they used to. Life is more stagnant. Or worse, maybe they've experienced a few losses, a few disappointments, a few embarrassments.

We tend to respond to these seasons in one of a couple different ways. We may react with *despondency*, growing indifferent to the world and assuming the previous seasons of excitement and fervor were just hype. Then we become cynical. Or we may try to re-create previous circumstances. Let's call that *nostalgia*. We seek out a new season of excitement, a new church, a new spiritual experience, a new conference, a new adventure, or maybe even a new spouse, looking for that original spark of life. We try to make something happen again. Anything!

In times of stagnancy, I encourage you to resist both despondency and nostalgia. These moments demand a level of maturity. Earlier in our faith, God moved in exciting seasons, giving us major and obvious witnesses of his presence and power.

We could see them and believe. But now we are called to see and give witness to God at work in quiet moments. "You see me in the exciting moments," he says to us, "but can you see me in the stillness or disappointment?"

Waiting on God

In a performative world, voices speak deep into our hearts about who we ought to be and what we ought to think about ourselves. These voices nestle into our subconscious and govern our choices and lives. In his wisdom, God knows we don't need another experience to excite us; we need *his voice* to heal us. We often need these stagnant seasons of grace to sit still enough to hear his voice over the voices of our circumstances, our desires, our busyness, our grief, our shame, our wounds, and our insecurities.

Jesus appears to his disciples, not in a thunderclap, but in a quiet moment over breakfast. Jesus doesn't disrupt the stagnant moment with excitement; he enters the moment and participates in it. This is a hard lesson to learn.

It's like the story of the prophet Elijah in 1 Kings 18–19. In chapter 18, we read that God used Elijah to confront the idolatry and false worship of Israel. Jezebel, the queen, was leading the nation toward the worship of Baal with her false prophets. In a moment of heightened confrontation between Elijah and Jezebel with her prophets on top of Mount Carmel, Elijah humiliated his enemies, showing how pitiful Baal was compared to the God of Israel. It was a public display of power before the watching world—a literal mountaintop experience of triumph for Elijah.

He was on the winning side. The Lord came through. Elijah was on top, at the peak of his career.

Until he wasn't. Jezebel wasn't going to stand for being humiliated. So she promised Elijah she would destroy him.

Suddenly the tables turned. Elijah was toast. He went on the run, wandering in the wilderness. He was depressed. He couldn't imagine a hopeful future. In a moment of exhaustion and despondency, Elijah asked if the Lord would just take his life: "It is enough; now, O LORD, take away my life" (1 Kings 19:4). He wanted to die. "I am no better than my fathers."

That statement—"I am no better than my fathers"—is about his previous experiences of triumph. Rebellious generations prior to him didn't trust in the Lord's provision and sought out false idols for help, undergoing God's punishment as a result. But now, Elijah, after resisting the idolatry of his fathers, was still experiencing what felt like punishment from the Lord. What good was it to give his life to such things if it wasn't going to benefit him? Maybe previous seasons of excitement and fervor were just hype. Jezebel's threats were all-consuming. In Elijah's exhaustion and depression, cynicism rose to the surface.

Remember, we often respond to seasons of stagnancy with either despondency or nostalgia. Here we see Elijah is no different. We can easily imagine nostalgia being an impulse as well, a longing to go back to the mountaintop experience of success and spiritual power.

But just like in the story of Peter, God was present. He led Elijah to another mountaintop, Horeb (1 Kings 19:8), in order to minister to him and care for him. He allowed Elijah to sleep and eat. Then God sent Elijah four things.

First, he sent a "strong wind" (1 Kings 19:11), a storm, like when God confronted Job in a whirlwind to explain the injustices and sufferings of the world (Job 38:1). Surely God would speak from out of the wind and thunder to stir and strengthen Elijah. But, the text says, "the LORD was not in the wind."

After the wind came an earthquake, like back in Numbers 16, when the earth shook and swallowed up the enemies of Moses and the Israelites in order to display the power of the Lord. That's what Elijah needed, right? His enemies were great, and maybe the Lord would come through again by dropping them into a chasm. But, the text says, "the LORD was not in the earthquake" (1 Kings 19:11).

And after the earthquake, a fire. Yes, the fire of God's presence was just what Elijah needed, like the pillar of fire that led the Israelites through the wilderness and the fire that lit the top of Mount Sinai (Exodus 13:21; 19:18). Surely Elijah longed for a dramatic display of God's presence. But, the text says, "the LORD was not in the fire" (1 Kings 19:12).

Finally, after the wind, the earthquake, and the fire, God sent a "low whisper." His voice and presence were in that still, small voice. Elijah didn't need the spiritual mountaintop experiences of a hurricane, earthquake, or fire. He needed to be quiet long enough that the voice of God could speak louder to his heart than Jezebel's threats. This is why God tells us in the Psalms, "Be still, and know that I am God" (Psalm 46:10). Let me speak louder to your heart than the world around you, he says. Let me speak louder than the voice of your parents. Let me speak louder than social media. Let me speak louder than the voice of your supervisors and coworkers. Let me speak louder than the promises of the world. Let me speak louder than the voice of your own heart that condemns you.

For a long life of confidence, hope, joy, and obedience, both Elijah and Peter needed something deeper than the seasons of excitement and triumph. We do too. Seasons of stagnancy summon us to spiritual maturity and demand that we resist the performative temptation to *make something happen*. Be still, and look for the witness of God's presence.

The Little Things

Returning to the story told in John 21, Jesus met the disciples in their low moment of stagnancy and performed a miracle. He stood on the shore and watched his disciples struggle to catch fish. In his kindness, he yelled out to his friends, "Cast the net on the right side of the boat, and you will find some" (John 21:6). When they did, they brought in a haul almost too great to land.

Remember, this fish miracle happened in the Sea of Tiberias, the same place where Jesus performed another fish miracle back in John 6, when he multiplied a few pieces of fish and some bread to feed five thousand people. When John recorded this location, did he hope we'd notice?

And then another detail: They brought in *153* fish. Why not just say "a lot of fish"? Or just give a nice round number of 150? If you read commentaries on this text written throughout history, you'll see that interpreters have made a lot of creative efforts to find something symbolic in the number 153. But I wonder if this detail is communicating something more ordinary. Perhaps John is trying to get us to see that this moment happened to real people, in a real place, and in a real time in history.

These disciples existed in a *real* time—after the Feast of

Unleavened Bread—in a *real* place—by the Sea of Tiberias—with real, tangible details—153 fish. In other words, this story is a real thing that happens to real people—people like you and me. Jesus comes into these slow moments to meet us and bring healing. This didn't just happen to Peter; it happens to us. There is real spiritual potency in the "after this," mundane seasons of life. These are wilderness moments where God is slowly working things out in our hearts—things that require us to be patient.

In previous seasons of spiritual power and excitement, it's obvious where we can see God at work. Take the story I told at the beginning of this chapter about my friend who could point to real times of power and grace in his life. In those moments, he didn't have to look hard for God. But *stagnant* seasons are moments when God is drawing us out, inviting us to seek him more profoundly. Sure, you can find him when your life feels like fireworks, but can you seek him when it feels like the lights are going out?

This is an invitation to maturity. Don't miss it by trying to make something happen or by performing your way out of the season. Don't resent slow, ordinary seasons when nothing seems to be happening to you or for you. Pay attention to where God is present and grace is at work. Listen and look for what you might receive from him.

A Simple Meal

Then Jesus sat with Peter and the other disciples around a charcoal fire. You may not have noticed this detail the first time you read this story, but just a few days prior to this, Peter had warmed himself by another charcoal fire. It was a very different scene. Jesus had just been arrested, and most of his disciples had fled. Peter followed a safe distance behind, wanting to see what would happen. The soldiers took Jesus to see the high priest, and Peter waited outside with a group of people who were warming themselves by a fire. Around that fire, three times someone asked Peter if he was associated with Jesus. Three times Peter denied even knowing him. The rooster crowed, and Peter came to himself and "wept bitterly" (Matthew 26:75).

But between these two fires are the death and resurrection of Jesus. Peter's sins were forgiven and paid for. But there was still the need for healing and restoration.

Remember the woman in Mark 5:25–34 who suffered from bleeding that wouldn't stop, despite spending all of her money seeking a remedy? For twelve years she suffered. Jewish law would have regarded her as continuously unclean. The blood flow would have needed to stop for at least seven days before she could be considered clean again. For twelve years, she was alienated from spiritual community and unable to be touched, lest the other person become "unclean." How heartbreaking!

In a last-ditch effort, she secretly made her way through the crowds to touch the hem of Jesus' garment without being noticed. It was risky. She wasn't supposed to touch anything. But when she touched Jesus' garment, the flow of blood stopped and she was healed. Jesus paused amid the crowds to announce that he had been touched and power had gone out of him. The woman finally came forward and identified herself. Jesus could have quickly moved on to heal someone else in urgent need of care. But he stopped, looked at the woman, and spoke a word of peace to her.

There are two moments of healing in this story: the woman's

physical healing from Jesus' touch and her *full* healing from his attention. If I can risk using this story in a paradigmatic way, consider this: Peter was forgiven at the cross. That was his first healing. Without question, he certainly needed that after his denials. But Jesus didn't ascend to heaven before providing Peter with a second healing. Peter also needed to be made whole again. His forgiveness came from the cross, but his wholeness came from Jesus' presence.

These moments of wholeness often come in stagnant seasons, and we should welcome them without resistance. They don't come in the wind, the earthquake, or the fire; they come in the moments when we are quiet enough to hear God's voice and still enough to see his face. If you take anything away from this book, I pray that you learn to grow out of a performative life into one that is nonanxious enough to engage in these moments with a quiet, healing Jesus.

Around a fire, Jesus has breakfast with Peter. Notice two important details from this scene. First, *Jesus meets with Peter around a charcoal fire*—a reminder of Peter's sin, failure, and embarrassment. Jesus is bringing the pain of this failure to the surface. He's not letting Peter bury it. He's going to have to confront what happened. You can't help but sense the pain in this encounter.

Second, *this is a meal.* You don't have to read much of the New Testament Gospels to notice how much Jesus ministers his grace over meals. Meals are invitations to friendship. They are for intimates, not enemies. This is a setting of restoration, not condemnation. This is a safe place for Peter.

It's all here. The charcoal fire is a reminder of *sin*, but the meal is a reminder of *grace*. This is how Jesus brings restoration. He doesn't ignore sin, sweeping it under the rug. He brings it to the surface, allowing difficult emotions to emerge—all the things that bring regret, embarrassment, shame, and guilt. He brings them out into the light. But again, Jesus never brings up anything he doesn't intend to heal. This is a mercy. We, like Peter, often aren't quick (or even able) to do the work ourselves. And sin and shame work most powerfully when unacknowledged and covered up. They are most dangerous in the dark. So Jesus uncovers them—gently, restoratively, like a friend working through reconciliation over breakfast.

This kind of work cannot be done in seasons of hurry. It happens in the "after this" seasons—in seasons of quiet, when nothing is *happening*—when by God's grace we resist trying to *make something happen.*

I don't want to idealize certain seasons over others. There may be times when you are called to fill your days with action and move at a pace that only God can give you energy to maintain. And sometimes, those who prioritize "stillness" are really only reaching for sloth or comfort.

But it's worth remembering that Jesus, over and over, emphasizes seasons when our lives are more hidden than public. So much deep work can be accomplished in those times. And since our human hearts tend to resist what is hidden for what is seen, what is secret for what is public, it's important to consider these things more closely.

"More Than These"

Three times Jesus asks Peter, "Do you love me?" But the first time, he asks, "Do you love me *more than these*?" (John 21:15).

At first you might wonder if Jesus is asking, "Do you love me more than these fish?" In other words, "Do you love fishing more than what I've called you to?" But that's not what Jesus has in mind here. He will get to recommissioning Peter back to the mission to which Jesus has called him, but first he must ask Peter a deeper question: "Do you love me more than the other disciples love me?"

Now, Jesus isn't asking, "Who loves me most?" He's alluding to a previous moment in John 13, when Jesus told the disciples he would be arrested and then every one of his disciples would abandon him. Peter, full of pride and confidence and passion, said, "Lord . . . I will lay down my life for you" (John 13:37). In Matthew's gospel, he's much more flagrant in his boasts: "Though they all fall away because of you, I will never fall away" (Matthew 26:33). Peter elevates himself above the other disciples as one who will never fail but will be characterized by exceptional loyalty. But now, after Peter's abysmal denials, Jesus addresses the pride and self-confidence: "Do you still think you love me more than these?"

Jesus isn't humiliating Peter. He's bringing up a painful example of his pride. It's not simply to prove he was right when he told Peter he would deny him (John 13:38); it's to point out the thing that kept Peter from staying with Jesus in moments of stress and threat. Jesus knows there will be moments ahead in Peter's life that will once again call for his faithfulness and perseverance. Something deeper than pride and zeal will be needed in these moments, since those very things failed him around the first charcoal fire.

In moments like this, Jesus is addressing the things that hinder us from staying or persevering with him. What are the wounds that make us cynical? The idols that distract us? The fears that keep us distant? The guilt that makes us hide? The shame that reaches for a mask?

For Peter, pride and self-sufficiency were what kept him from love. And in this "after this" moment, Peter is likely wrestling with the shame of not living up to the faithfulness he boasted about. Pride mixed with shame has a way of producing either a more hardened, "prove yourself" mentality or a weakened will that keeps you from giving yourself to anything meaningful again. Jesus had a better future in mind for Peter, but not without first addressing his pride and shame.

Peter must grasp an important lesson: his own passion, zeal, and energy are not reliable sources for perseverance and lasting love. Notice that Peter doesn't say, "Yes, Lord. I do love you. I'm committed. I'm there 100 percent! You can count on me. I'm all in!" Peter must embody a different posture here in this moment and from now on. His answer shows that he understands his need to grasp for something deeper than his own passion and zeal.

In fact, in answering Jesus' question—"Do you love me more than these?"—Peter doesn't even refer to himself at all. He doesn't say, "Lord, I know I failed you, but *I can do better.*" Instead, he answers, "Yes, Lord; you *know* that I love you" (John 21:15, emphasis added). In other words, when trying to give evidence of his love, he cannot appeal to his own convictions or his own zeal. They have not been trustworthy measures. He can only appeal to Jesus. *Lord, you know my heart.*

I find this to be remarkably comforting. I've experienced seasons when my own actions and desires have confused me. I've allowed my ambitions and plans to get in the way of relationships. I remember a particular season of stress when decisions for the future of our church needed to be made. I was both excited and anxious. At the same time, one of our leaders was experiencing deep weakness and needed my attention. Looking back now, I can see that the urgency of making decisions for the church was fueled more by my anxiety and ambitions than by the reality of the circumstance. But what I found myself feeling was that my friend in weakness was an obstacle to my desires rather than an object of my love and attention. Remembering this causes me grief and embarrassment. As the apostle Paul said about his own heart, "I do not understand my own actions" (Romans 7:15).

Peter was surprised at his ability to deny knowing Jesus so easily. But Jesus wasn't. There are times when "Lord, you know" might be all we can say. And yet it's a good response from Peter. He is trusting in whatever Jesus knows about him. It may not be flattering, but it hasn't kept Jesus from loving him.

Jesus knew Peter's heart, but he didn't treat him on the basis of his failure. Jesus has a future-orientated posture toward Peter. Peter's denials and pride will not have the last word about him. Jesus is summoning him to a greater life. But Peter will have to learn to depend on things deeper than his passion and zeal.

I wonder if some of us need to digest this truth more deeply for ourselves. Indeed, in the New Testament, there are places that call us to be passionate and zealous for Christ (see Romans 12:8). But at other times, passion and zeal will not be sufficient for perseverance and lasting love.

For most of my life, growing up and into young adulthood, I was characterized by a kind of passion and zeal that sustained me through a lot of difficult circumstances. Both Jena and I were able to grind our way through seasons we didn't enjoy because we knew better things were most likely coming on the other side. We tended to stick with things even when they got tough because we were passionate about what we felt called to do.

Maybe this describes you. You have a tenacity and level of perseverance that allows you to stick with things and fight your way through. We tend to interpret this "strength" through a spiritual lens. When others falter in times of stress or trouble, we grow more confident in our own spiritual strength, echoing Peter: "Though they all fall away because of you, I will never fall away" (Matthew 26:33).

For those of us tempted to think this way, may I suggest that our ability to grind it out longer than others might come more from our temperament or personality than from spiritual strength? For example, maybe somewhere along the line you were programmed to fear failure, so you persevere longer. Or perhaps the objective you're laboring for is inordinately important to you, thereby pushing you past healthy limitations. Or maybe, for physiological or psychological reasons, you have more energy in this season of life than other people do.

From ages eighteen to thirty-five, I had a passion and focus that drove me to persevere and overcome in difficult seasons. But I learned that I wasn't the same person at the age of thirty-seven that I was at twenty-seven. I'm no longer driven by the same desires; I no longer possess the same energy or focus.

At twenty-seven, I was a young dad who had a lot of optimism and energy. No meaningful doors had been closed in my face. I had ideas and ambitions informed by zero experience. I could run on very little sleep, eat anything I wanted, and be clearheaded and competent in what I was trying to accomplish. At thirty-seven, I was more seasoned. I had teenagers. I had experienced meaningful failure and heartache. I was caught off guard by regular and seasonal depression that demanded that I take my limitations seriously, get enough sleep, eat healthy foods, and exercise regularly.

As with Peter, my zeal and passion that I interpreted as spiritual strengths were perhaps more temperamental and physiological than I had imagined. And there came a time in my life when I wasn't the same person. My previous zeal and passion weren't serving me in times of loss, disappointment, depression, embarrassment, or failure. It's in those kinds of moments that we learn whether our obedience and perseverance are from a performative spirituality or from a deep spiritual strength. I've had my own "charcoal fire" moments when Jesus confronted me about what I was depending on for a long life of obedience and lasting love. And you need those moments too.

Complete Restoration

After Jesus asks Peter—not just once, but three times—"Peter, do you love me?" there's no more wondering. Jesus certainly is making a point. And we can see that Peter feels wounded from his words:

"Do you love me?"

"Yes, you know I love you."

"Do you love me?"

"Yes, you know I love you."

"Do you love me?"

"Lord, you know all things!"

At first glance, this seems harsh. Is Jesus pushing too far?

Why not just ask one direct question and simply say, "I forgive you"? Why draw the drama out?

In the Bible, the number "three" embodies a sense of completeness. God is not just *holy* in Isaiah 6—he is *holy, holy, holy*. So Jesus is doing something intentional with Peter. Remember the three times Peter disowned Christ: "I do not know what you mean; I do not know the man; I do not know the man" (Matthew 26:69–75). Peter can't even say his name. Jesus is just "the man." Three times he denies knowing Jesus. *Complete* rejection. I imagine Peter feared that his denial and sin defined him.

So Jesus drew Peter out three times, as if to say, "My restoration will be as thorough as your denial. My restoration will have the last word about you, not your sin." You can sense from the narrative that Peter felt the embarrassment and pain of his sin. That's certainly part of it. But by the time breakfast was done, he felt the joy of forgiveness and wholeness.

Here's the confidence those of us in Christ can have: Restoration and healing will have the last word about us. As Peter was eating the fish, he was digesting forgiveness. It probably reshaped the way he experienced charcoal fires. Maybe instead of bringing up difficult emotions of shame, they brought to mind the warmth of God's grace, mercy, and kindness. In this painful but intimate moment, Jesus healed and transformed Peter. Seemingly stagnant moments hold the potential to do the same for us as well. It can be *our* story.

CONCLUSION

In Luke's gospel, Jesus' disciples have both a story of success and a story of failure in their encounters with unclean spirits. The *failure story* is told in Luke 9. Jesus enters an already intense scene, where a man has been begging the disciples to heal his son, who is being tormented by an unclean spirit. But they can't do it. Jesus rebukes the spirit and heals the son, leaving everyone amazed (Luke 9:37–43). Mark's gospel unpacks the scene in more detail, especially as the disciples express confusion over their failure. "Why could we not cast it out?" they ask. "This kind," Jesus says, "cannot be driven out by anything but prayer" (Mark 9:28–29).

The *success story* comes soon afterward. It's a narrative we considered back in chapter 2—from Luke 10. Jesus sends the disciples out on a mission to the surrounding areas to preach the gospel and heal the sick. When they come back, they report huge successes. No details are given other than, "Lord, even the demons are subject to us in your name!" (Luke 10:17). Now, I can't be sure of it, but I wonder if they cared about this detail because they clearly remembered their previous failure with demons. Maybe it had demoralized their hearts. "Why could we not cast it out?" But now some sense of confidence is back, and they're feeling better about themselves.

Jesus' response is encouraging as well: "I saw Satan fall like lightning from heaven" (Luke 10:18). Their work isn't simply a moment of a few demons being overcome. Jesus is putting their triumph in the context of Satan's defeat. Their mission is to participate in and experience a foretaste of Jesus' ultimate triumph over Satan's reign in the world. I can't imagine better feedback. I get all kinds of responses to my sermons on Sunday—some good, some bad. But never do I hear, *While you were preaching, I saw Satan fall like lightning.*

This is an inspiring moment for Jesus' followers. The disciples experience success, and Jesus promises them that more success is coming: "I have given you authority to tread on serpents and scorpions, and over all the power of the enemy, and nothing shall hurt you" (Luke 10:19). This is a far cry from earlier days, when they were helpless against the demon possessing the young boy. The future looked bright.

But Jesus sees into their hearts and knows where they could misplace their trust: "Nevertheless, do not rejoice in this, that the spirits are subject to you, but rejoice that your names are written in heaven" (Luke 10:20). Jesus is concerned that they were beginning to place the weight of their sense of significance on their outward success. So he is pointing them to where their names are written—somewhere in a secret place far from the eyes of others and hidden from the notice of the world. Let me show you, he says, where the substance of who you are truly resides.

Consider what Jesus is saying. *You are neither who you thought you were when you couldn't cast out the demons, nor who you think you are now, after Satan fell like lightning.*[1]

We tend to identify ourselves either by our outward successes or by our humiliating failures because these outward displays of our competencies, beauty, achievements, taste, togetherness—or lack of these things—are where we feel most loved and accepted, or most judged and forgotten, by others. We have based our sense of well-being in the performative parts of our lives. As a result, we often experience our lives as fragile.

Jesus leads his disciples and us into a deeper place of being, not in our public displays of competence, but in the secret place of thunder with the Father, where our names are written and will never be erased. But as we've seen, to follow these words, we must follow Jesus along a path that feels like death.

The most famous way Jesus describes this *death-life* is his call to his disciples in Mark's gospel: "If anyone would come after me, let him deny himself and take up his cross and follow me. For whoever would save his life will lose it, but whoever loses his life for my sake and the gospel's will save it" (Mark 8:34–35). If you want to *live* with me, Jesus says, you must *die* with me. You must die to the ways of living that governed and characterized your life beforehand.

If you want to continue on with Jesus, from this day onward, what are the things that must die? What needs to fall from your life and decay so that life with Jesus can continue fruitfully and joyfully?

This call demands that we reconsider the things we have reached for when we've longed for acceptance, safety, beauty, or love. There was a couple in our church community known for their competency with money. Despite the suspicion that Manhattan is a place that seems to empty people of their money, this couple always seemed to know how to save, even with very ordinary levels of income. They prized their reputation as "good stewards." They even taught a class in our church on financial stewardship.

But now, after a few seasons of financial stress and loss, they've articulated how they look back at their previous selves less as "good stewards" and more as skillful at anxiously keeping money in case things went badly. They created systems so they would never *have* to trust in God for their daily bread. They realized they were never truly generous. They only gave when it was safe, never when it was sacrificial. Their system of safety kept them feeling okay when they desperately wanted to never feel needy.

What are the safety schemes and salvation plans you are reaching for? The deeper and more difficult question Jesus demands we ask is, *If I continue on in the life I am living now, will that be the life I want?*

Notice, I'm not asking if your safety schemes and salvation plans *work*. For some of you, they may be working great for now. We're often very good at finding ways of getting on in this world in order to experience a sense of love or success. Maybe you're very popular in this world—a lot of people like you—and it feels good. Maybe your plans have worked in getting you to the places you've wanted to be. Maybe you have the relationships and networks and career path you always hoped you'd have. Even if all these things are true, my question is different: *If your life were to continue on this trajectory, would it be the life you want?*

We Lack One Thing

I wish this question was penetrating enough and provoked such clarity that it allowed you to see through all the false promises of our Babylonian world and follow Christ more completely rather than performatively from now on. But it doesn't always work that way. For example, consider Jesus' encounter with the rich young man (Mark 10:17–22). This man came to Jesus longing for a deeper, more satisfying life. "What must I do to inherit eternal life?" he asked. Jesus began at the surface level, saying in effect, "You know the moral commandments of God. Do you follow those?" And the young man affirmed that he followed the commandments and was living a moral life.

Then the passage tells us, "Jesus, looking at him, loved him, and said to him, 'You lack one thing: go, sell all that you have and give to the poor, and you will have treasure in heaven; and come, follow me'" (Mark 10:21). Jesus looked at him and loved him. Jesus looked deeply, with compassion, into this man's life and saw all the ways he had tried to feel safe and admired in the world: through his riches. Jesus looked and loved the man and, with a tender heart, saw how fragile his life was. Of course his life was fragile! Why would he be standing in front of Jesus, asking for something more, if it wasn't fragile?

So Jesus said, "You lack one thing: go, sell all that you have and give to the poor, and you will have treasure in heaven; and come, follow me." Jesus knew that if this man's life were to continue on its current path, it wouldn't be the life he wanted. But Jesus pointed out that in order for this man to get the life he longed for, he would have to die to his salvation plans and safety schemes. He would have to die to his wealth. In the end, however, the young man refused the offer. It was too risky. He wanted Jesus *on top of* his riches and impressiveness. He knew his wealth wasn't enough to satisfy him, but he also couldn't imagine a life without it.

But we don't know the end of this young man's story. Maybe there was something about the way Jesus loved him that he couldn't shake. Maybe one day, when this young man wasn't so young anymore, he came to the end of himself and saw that his wealth could not give him what Jesus' look of love had offered him. Maybe he would hear of the way Jesus died, how he gave up his divine and heavenly wealth to love, not just the world generally, but him personally. We'll never know. But I wonder if we put ourselves in the place of this rich young man and receive what Jesus has to say, we might respond, "Yes, I'll do as you say, and I'll follow you, Jesus," and walk into a deeper and more joyful way of living rather than turning away sad.

Just as he did with the rich young man, Jesus looks at us and loves us. He sees with his searching eyes the things that keep us frail, fragile, and distant from his presence. And he asks us, "If your life continues on in the way it's going, is this the life you want?"

And with a tender voice, he continues: "These things must die in order that you might live." This is a word of love for us. But it's also one that demands a sober reckoning, because death feels like death.

We read the story of the rich young man in the Gospels and often consider it a story of a potential conversion. Are you going to begin a new life with Christ today, or will you reject him forever? Forever saved or an eternal sinner? And, yes, it can be understood that way. But this encounter with Jesus—who looks and loves, who asks us to willingly die to the Babylonian promises of this world and follow him—is a daily labor. When we wake up and spend a few moments in the morning preparing to follow Jesus for the next sixteen hours or so, he looks at our hearts with love and says, "You lack one thing."

That one thing is the death and burial of what we are trusting in and hoping for that keeps us from experiencing and following Jesus. That death and burial isn't a onetime event at the beginning of our faith or the dramatic moment of repentance from some deep, dark sin in our Christian life. *It is the Christian life.*

A Life of Paschal Death

These death and burial experiences are hard because moving away from a performative life can actually bring on things we fear—going unnoticed, looking unimpressive, or being found out. We may lose opportunities for a kind of connectivity that we think our goals depend on. These deaths will *feel* like death. And we are taught to resist them with all our might.

Our Babylonian, performative world says that the loss of money, comfort, job potential, sexual fulfillment, and reputation is as good as death—a *terminal* death. If you don't have these things or aren't able to pursue them, it's not a life worth living.

But Christianity has always made a distinction between *terminal* death and what we might call a *paschal* death.[2] The word *paschal* comes from the language of the sacrificial Passover lamb, when the Israelites celebrated their deliverance from Egypt. On the night the angel of the Lord killed all the firstborn in Egypt, any family that put the blood of a lamb on their doorposts would be spared (Exodus 12:13). The paschal lamb saved them. Jesus is called "the Lamb of God" (John 1:29)—the ultimate Paschal Lamb. He died, and we were saved by his blood. He died that we might have life with him.

Here, then, is the distinction between a *terminal death* and a *paschal death*: Terminal death is a death that ends life and ends possibilities. Maybe it's your literal biological life, or maybe it's the thing you protect and love so much that to lose it means the end of any meaningful continuation of life. Paschal death, on the other hand, is a death that, while ending or losing one kind of life, opens a second form of life—deeper and richer than before. Grain is buried in the ground as in a tomb and dies. But then it grows into a new, transformed life. It's a generative death.

The challenging thing about these lives of paschal deaths is that they are often unknown. These are quite different lives than the famous lives of sacrifice that we know of because of some public vindication in the end. Often we don't hear about them unless we get to witness them ourselves. One of these kinds of lives belongs to a leader in our church who works in the finance industry in New York City—a brutal industry that can absolutely eat up the lives of individuals and families. On the way to advancement, you will get money, access, and success, but you will lose so much in the process.

However, my friend decided to resist this path and has chosen to remain in a still demanding yet sustainable position in his firm. He has undoubtedly lost a particular kind of reputation and significant amounts of money. He doesn't have access and invitations to certain kinds of circles that are promised to him if he would just give himself to this world. By choosing a different path, he has allowed himself to be present and sacrificial to the community he loves. Yet here is the double wound: Nobody in our community—other than me and a few others, like his spouse—knows what he has died to in order to be present. His firm's widely circulated newsletter isn't going to boast in the intentional limitations he has chosen at work in order to be present to his church community. Nor is my friend going to boast in his paschal deaths along the way. He is simply trusting in what his Father in heaven sees, and that's enough.

I suggest this is a good life that we ought to pursue with holy ambition.

Remember the story in John 21 of Peter and Jesus sitting around a charcoal fire? We ended that story in the previous chapter with Jesus reconciling with Peter by asking him three times if he loved him. But there's a little more to the story. Immediately after this, Jesus says to Peter, "Truly, truly, I say to you, when you were young, you used to dress yourself and walk wherever you wanted, but when you are old, you will stretch out your hands, and another will dress you and carry you where you do not want to go" (John 21:18).

Jesus tells Peter how he will die and how he will live. From Christian tradition, we know that Peter was martyred in the way described above—captured and crucified, like Jesus was. But this statement is also in the context of Jesus' call to Peter to follow him. John 21:18 is a description of what Peter's following would look like.

It's also what life will look like for us when we die to our old life so we may live in Christ. When we were young, before we knew Jesus, we lived how we wanted and went where we wanted to go, but now with Christ, we must die to that life, giving it away for something deeper than just our own ambitions and desires. And Jesus offers us some provocative imagery to help us understand this experience: "You will stretch out your hands, and another will dress you and carry you where you do not want to go" (John 21:18).

When we were born, we were highly vulnerable. We were desperately linked to and in need of our parents for everything.

We needed food, clothing, safety, and a place to feel at home. We had nothing of our own. But as we grew, we transitioned into a new way of being where we began to clothe ourselves, accumulate our own things, and distinguish ourselves from our parents and those who provided for us. We began to grow toward separation and self-actualization. We became our own person with our own plans and vision for life as an individual person. And the Bible says this is a good thing. At some point, we leave our parents (see Genesis 2:24).

Our world teaches us that the self-actualization project shouldn't stop there. It should keep going toward a life of prioritizing *my* needs and ambitions, *my* comfort and success. It's a radical vision of freedom and individualism, which we've seen leads to the frailty of a performative life. But God asks something different of us. Instead of following the patterns of a self-protective and self-curating world, we're called to follow the pattern of Christ's sacrificial and self-giving love with others. He asks us to stretch out our hands in the act of crucifying our lives—and the longing to be seen and admired—to be taken to a place where we'd rather not go (at least for now): a hidden place of love with the Father.

Our society has taught us to believe that the good life should be seen as free and beautiful. But it's a trap. This kind of life, says Christopher Lasch, has a devastating effect on the second half of life and brings with it the certainty of terrible suffering ahead: "In a society that dreads old age and death, aging holds a special terror for those who fear dependence and whose self-esteem requires the admiration usually reserved for youth, beauty, celebrity, or charm."[3]

Instead of continuing on in our individual projects of self-actualization, Jesus calls us to give of ourselves. Instead of distinguishing ourselves against others, we give ourselves to others and receive what others give to us. This life of self-giving can happen only when we are vulnerable and known, first in secret with the Father and then in love with others. It's a life that embraces the "clothes" that Jesus gives to Peter—someone else "will dress you and carry you where you do not want to go."

Those clothes are the life of paschal death. It's a death that produces a new life, new fruit, new joys, new zeal, and a larger heart. It's the path toward maturity. It will help you age and die well. No book has the power to create that transformation in you. But I hope this one has provoked an imagination and a longing for what Christ might have for you on the other side of a performative life.

NOTES

NOTES

Introduction

1. Robert N. Bellah et al., *Habits of the Heart: Individualism and Commitment in American Life* (Berkeley: University of California Press, 1985), 27.

2. Thomas Curran and Andrew P. Hill, "Perfectionism Is Increasing over Time: A Meta-analysis of Birth Cohort Differences from 1989 to 2016," *Psychological Bulletin* 145, no. 4 (2019): 420, emphasis mine, www.apa.org/pubs/journals/releases/bul-bul0000138.pdf.

3. See Sophie Gilbert, "Millennial Burnout Is Being Televised," *Atlantic*, January 22, 2019, www.theatlantic.com/entertainment/archive/2019/01/marie-kondo-fyre-fraud-and-tvs-millennial-burnout/580753.

4. Gilbert, "Millennial Burnout Is Being Televised."

5. Curran and Hill, "Perfectionism Is Increasing over Time," 412.

6. Curran and Hill, "Perfectionism Is Increasing over Time," 413.

7. See Murray W. Enns, Brian J. Cox, and Ian P. Clara, "Perfectionism and Neuroticism: A Longitudinal Study of Specific Vulnerability and Diathesis-Stress Models," *Cognitive Therapy and Research* 29, no. 4 (August 2005): 463–78.

8. Yuval Levin, *A Time to Build: From Family and Community to Congress and the Campus, How Recommitting to Our Institutions Can Revive the American Dream* (New York: Basic Books, 2020), 33–34.

9. Edwin H. Friedman, *A Failure of Nerve: Leadership in the Age of the Quick Fix*, rev. ed. (New York: Church Publishing, 2017), 253.

Chapter 1: Performative Spirituality

1. Quoted in Anne Helen Petersen, "I Just Think This Idea of Being Young and Carefree No Longer Applies to Our Current Reality. I Feel Old and Weary," Culture Study, March 10, 2021, https://annehelen.substack.com/p/i-just-think-the-idea-of-being -young.

2. See Terry Nguyễn, "The Class of 2020 Was Full of Hope. Then the Pandemic Hit," *Vox*, December 9, 2020, www.vox.com/the -goods/22158622/youth-unemployment-rate.

3. Anne Helen Petersen, "How Millennials Became the Burnout Generation," BuzzFeed News, January 5, 2019, www.buzzfeed news.com/article/annehelenpetersen/millennials-burnout -generation-debt-work.

4. Sophie Gilbert, "Millennial Burnout Is Being Televised," *Atlantic*, January 22, 2019, www.theatlantic.com/entertainment /archive/2019/01/marie-kondo-fyre-fraud-and-tvs-millennial -burnout/580753.

5. Thomas Curran and Andrew P. Hill, "Perfectionism Is Increasing over Time: A Meta-analysis of Birth Cohort Differences from 1989 to 2016," *Psychological Bulletin* 145, no. 4 (2019): 420, www.apa.org/pubs/journals/releases/bul-bul0000138.pdf.

6. Petersen, "How Millennials Became the Burnout Generation," italics in original.

7. This truth summarizes what David Benner talks about in his book *The Gift of Being Yourself: The Sacred Call to Self-Discovery*, rev. ed. (Downers Grove, IL: InterVarsity, 2015), 69–82.

8. Benner, *Gift of Being Yourself*, 25, emphasis mine.

9. Frederick Dale Bruner, *The Christbook: Matthew 1–12*, vol. 1 of *Matthew: A Commentary*, rev. ed. (Grand Rapids: Eerdmans, 2004), 285.

Chapter 2: A Hidden Life

1. Jeffrey Anderson, "Movie Review: A Hidden Life," Common Sense Media, www.commonsensemedia.org/movie-reviews/a -hidden-life, accessed August 15, 2022.

2. See D. A. Carson, "Matthew," in vol. 8 of *The Expositor's Bible Commentary* (Grand Rapids: Zondervan, 2006), 317–18.

3. Quoted in The School of Life, *The School of Life: An Emotional Education* (London: Penguin, 2020), 42–43.

4. Annie Dillard, *Teaching a Stone to Talk: Expeditions and Encounters* (1982; repr., New York: HarperPerennial, 1992), 49.

5. Thomas Merton, *The Silent Life* (1957; repr., New York: Farrar, Straus and Giroux, 1999), 14–15.

6. Quoted in Will Storr, *Selfie: How We Became So Self-Obsessed and What It's Doing to Us* (New York: Overlook, 2018), 15–16.

7. See "Suicidal Thoughts, Suicide Attempts, and Self-Harm," chapter 12 in *Adult Psychiatric Morbidity Survey: Survey of Mental Health and Wellbeing, England, 2014*, NHS Digital, September 29, 2016, https://digital.nhs.uk/data-and-information /publications/statistical/adult-psychiatric-morbidity-survey/adult -psychiatric-morbidity-survey-survey-of-mental-health-and -wellbeing-england-2014, accessed August 15, 2022.

8. Thomas Curran and Andrew P. Hill, "Perfectionism Is Increasing over Time: A Meta-analysis of Birth Cohort Differences from 1989 to 2016," *Psychological Bulletin* 145, no. 4 (2019): 412, www.apa.org/pubs/journals/releases/bul-bul0000138.pdf.

9. Cited in Storr, *Selfie*, 12.

10. Martin M. Smith et al., "The Perniciousness of Perfectionism: A Meta-analytical Review of the Perfectionism-Suicide Relationship," *Journal of Personality* 86, no. 3 (June 2018): 522–42, www.researchgate.net/publication/318381042_The _perniciousness_of_perfectionism_A_meta-analytic_review_of _the_perfectionism-suicide_relationship.

11. Modern translations cut out the word *fasting* since it was probably a later addition to manuscripts when the practice of fasting was becoming more commonly practiced among Christians. But I do think the inclusion of fasting does grasp the sense of what Jesus is telling his disciples. It's the hidden habits—the Matthew 6 path of giving to the poor, praying, and fasting in secret—that are needed.

Chapter 3: Fruitful Dormancy

1. Thomas Curran and Andrew P. Hill, "Perfectionism Is Increasing over Time: A Meta-analysis of Birth Cohort Differences from 1989 to 2016," *Psychological Bulletin* 145, no. 4 (2019): 420, www.apa.org/pubs/journals/releases/bul-bul0000138.pdf.

2. Curran and Hill, "Perfectionism Is Increasing over Time," 420.

3. Curran and Hill, "Perfectionism Is Increasing over Time," 420, emphasis mine.

4. Jean Twenge, *Generation Me: Why Today's Young Americans Are More Confident, Assertive, Entitled—and More Miserable Than Ever Before* (New York: Free Press, 2006), 52–68.

5. Curran and Hill, "Perfectionism Is Increasing over Time," 410.

6. Pew Research shows that as most millennials are reaching their forties, more than 45 percent of them are not living with a family of their own. Compare this to Gen X, where only 34 percent at a similar stage in life were not living with a family of

their own. Further, only a third of millennial fathers are living with their own children: "Millennial men are less likely to be living in a household with their own children than was the case for previous generations of men at a comparable age" (Amanda Barroso, Kim Parker, and Jesse Bennett, "As Millennials Near 40, They're Approaching Family Life Differently Than Previous Generations," Pew Research Center, May 27, 2020, www.pew research.org/social-trends/2020/05/27/as-millennials-near-40 -theyre-approaching-family-life-differently-than-previous -generations).

7. See Fred Sanders, "A Welcome to the Plague (Samuel Shaw)," Scriptorium Daily, April 14, 2020, https://scriptoriumdaily.com /a-welcome-to-the-plague-samuel-shaw.

8. Quoted in Sanders, "Welcome to the Plague."

9. Quoted in Sanders, "Welcome to the Plague."

10. Alan Noble, *You Are Not Your Own: Belonging to God in an Inhuman World* (Downers Grove, IL: InterVarsity, 2021), 131.

11. Colleen Walsh, "Young Adults Hardest Hit by Loneliness during Pandemic," *Harvard Gazette*, February 17, 2021, https://news .harvard.edu/gazette/story/2021/02/young-adults-teens-loneliness -mental-health-coronavirus-covid-pandemic.

12. Mark E. Czeisler et al., "Mental Health, Substance Use, and Suicidal Ideation during the COVID-19 Pandemic—United States, June 24–30, 2020," *Morbidity and Mortality Weekly Report* 69, no. 42 (August 14, 2020): 1049–57, www.cdc.gov/mmwr /volumes/69/wr/mm6932a1.htm?s_cid=mm6932a1_w.

Chapter 4: Sowing Our Death

1. Anne Helen Petersen, "How Millennials Became the Burnout Generation," BuzzFeed News, January 5, 2019, www.buzzfeed

news.com/article/annehelenpetersen/millennials-burnout
-generation-debt-work.

2. L. M. Sacasas, "You Can't Optimize for Rest," *Convivial Society*,
December 1, 2021, https://theconvivialsociety.substack.com/p
/you-cant-optimize-for-rest.

3. Anne Helen Petersen, "How Our System Revenges Rest," *Culture
Study*, November 21, 2021, https://annehelen.substack.com/p/how
-our-system-revenges-rest.

4. Sacasas, "You Can't Optimize for Rest."

5. See Emma Beddington, "The Seven Types of Rest: I Spent
a Week Trying Them All. Could They Help End My
Exhaustion?" *Guardian*, November 25, 2021, www.theguardian
.com/lifeandstyle/2021/nov/25/the-seven-types-of-rest-i-spent
-a-week-trying-them-all-could-they-help-end-my-exhaustion.

6. David G. Benner, *The Gift of Being Yourself: The Sacred Call to
Self-Discovery* (Downers Grove, IL: InterVarsity, 2015), 51.

7. Benner, *Gift of Being Yourself*, 54.

8. Henri J. M. Nouwen, *The Wounded Healer* (New York: Image,
1979), 92.

9. Nouwen, *Wounded Healer*, 92.

10. Quoted in Joel Lovell, "The Late, Great Stephen Colbert," *GQ*,
August 17, 2015, www.gq.com/story/stephen-colbert-gq-cover
-story.

Chapter 5: Strategies for Joy

1. Curt Thompson, MD, *The Soul of Shame: Retelling the Stories We
Tell about Ourselves* (Downers Grove, IL: InterVarsity, 2015), 24,
italics in original.

2. Thompson, *Soul of Shame*, 44. To understand Thompson's larger
argument regarding the way shame impacts the entire mind and

its ability to make sense of our life, past, present, and future, see pages 37–55.

3. Thompson, *Soul of Shame*, 55.

4. Jonathan Haidt, "The Dangerous Experiment on Teen Girls," *Atlantic*, November 21, 2021, www.theatlantic.com/ideas /archive/2021/11/facebooks-dangerous-experiment-teen-girls /620767/.

5. Haidt, "Dangerous Experiment on Teen Girls."

6. Thompson, *Soul of Shame*, 42.

7. Thompson, *Soul of Shame*, 42.

8. Gordon D. Fee, *Paul, the Spirit, and the People of God* (Peabody, MA: Hendrickson, 1996), 11.

9. See Sophie Gilbert, "Millennial Burnout Is Being Televised," *Atlantic*, January 22, 2019, www.theatlantic.com/entertainment /archive/2019/01/marie-kondo-fyre-fraud-and-tvs-millennial -burnout/580753.

10. I wrote on what a secret life of prayer can look like in *The Possibility of Prayer: Finding Stillness with God in a Restless World* (Downers Grove, IL: InterVarsity, 2020).

11. Artur Weiser, *The Psalms: A Commentary* (Philadelphia: Westminster, 1962), 762.

12. A wonderful and powerful work on lament and grief is Todd J. Billings, *Rejoicing in Lament: Wrestling with Incurable Cancer and Life in Christ* (Grand Rapids: Brazos, 2015).

13. For psalms of personal lament, see Psalms 3, 6, 22, 28, 44, 56, 57, 71, 77, 142; for psalms of corporate lament, see Psalms 44, 60, 74, 79, 80, 85, 86, 90.

14. Eugene H. Peterson, *A Long Obedience in the Same Direction: Discipleship in an Instant Society*, 20th anniv. ed. (Downers Grove, IL: InterVarsity, 2000), 94.

Chapter 6: Abiding over Optimizing

1. Alexandra Schwartz, "Improving Ourselves to Death: What the Self-Help Gurus and Their Critics Reveal about Our Times," *New Yorker*, January 15, 2018, www.newyorker.com/magazine /2018/01/15/improving-ourselves-to-death.

2. Schwartz, "Improving Ourselves to Death."

3. Schwartz, "Improving Ourselves to Death."

4. See Will Storr, *Selfie: How We Became So Self-Obsessed and What It's Doing to Us* (New York: Overlook, 2018), 17.

5. Robert Letham, in his book *The Holy Trinity: In Scripture, History, Theology, and Worship* (Phillipsburg, NJ: P&R, 2004), includes a letter from Sinclair Ferguson that mentions this dynamic: "I've often reflected on the rather obvious thought that when his disciples were about to have the world collapse in on them, our Lord spent so much time in the Upper Room speaking to them about the mystery of the Trinity. If anything could underline the necessity of Trinitarianism for practical Christianity, that must surely be it!" (p. 375).

6. James K. A. Smith, *You Are What You Love: The Spiritual Power of Habit* (Grand Rapids: Brazos, 2016), 2.

Conclusion

1. This line is based loosely on a talk I heard given by Chuck DeGroat, who tells the story of a young priest who had early success in ministry but experienced failure soon thereafter.

2. See Ronald Rolheiser, *The Holy Longing: The Search for a Christian Spirituality* (New York: Doubleday, 1999), 146. Rolheiser takes this imagery in a different direction than I would, but he originally introduced me to these two categories of death.

3. Christopher Lasch, *The Culture of Narcissism: American Life in an Age of Diminishing Expectations* (New York: Norton, 1979), 41.